Prayer and the
Living Christ

Prayer and the Living Christ

FLORA SLOSSON WUELLNER

ABINGDON PRESS
NASHVILLE AND NEW YORK

PRAYER AND THE LIVING CHRIST

Copyright © 1969 by Abingdon Press

Library of Congress Catalog Card Number: 69-12015

SET UP, PRINTED, AND BOUND BY THE
PARTHENON PRESS, AT NASHVILLE,
TENNESSEE, UNITED STATES OF AMERICA

To my companions in prayer--
in the Church Militant and in the Church Triumphant

Contents

"From me as from a living fountain, the small and the great, the poor and the rich, do draw the water of life; and they that willingly and freely serve me shall receive grace for grace. . . .

"I have given thee all, and my will is to have thee all again. . . .

"I am he that has called thee; I have commanded it to be done; I will supply what is wanting in thee; come thou and receive me."

From *The Imitation of Christ*

Thomas à Kempis

Introduction

This book is written in anger and in gratitude.

It is a thrilling thing to be a member of the Christian church at this time. The new keen awareness of international, racial, and social justice, the thrust toward church unity, the experiments with liturgy, the new honest exploration of Christian thought and creed, the bold rethinking of parish organization are all dramatic developments that would have been almost inconceivable a generation ago.

Perhaps never before has the church been so varied in activity, so enriched with art and philosophy, or so engaged with social righteousness.

Nevertheless, the church is in danger. We are in very real danger of losing the foundation on which the church has been built. We are exulting over the fruit and the flower of the plant and ignoring its root. Never have we seemed so alive. Yet never have we been so detached from the source of our life.

Where is our Christ, who is alive and lives in power? In the preaching of our churches he has become a beautiful ideal. He has been turned into a myth, embodying a theological concept. The witness to his objective reality has largely been lost. Most liberal Protestant churches have never even heard of the prayer of power in his name. The church has become an organization of well-meaning, active idealists, working for Christ but far from his presence and his power.

In the average church, there will be twenty well-organized groups concerned with social, political, economic, educational problems, to perhaps one feebly struggling prayer group composed of five women and one man! Prayer is considered to be a pleasantly inspirational pastime. It does not occur to the average church to call on its praying members as a source of power. Rarely is the minister himself a man of great experience in prayer.

I have just finished reading through the 1967-68 course catalogues of twelve of our leading theological seminaries in the United States. Only six out of those twelve offer courses dealing specifically with the dynamics, disciplines, and literature of prayer. This does not refer to courses on liturgics or the history of Christian worship, but to courses on prayer itself as a need and a ministry of the individual and the congregation.

It is hoped, of course, and perhaps assumed that sooner or later each theological professor will discuss prayer in relation to his own discipline. It is also assumed that the whole of theological education deals at least indirectly with prayer. It is assumed that the two cannot be separated. Nevertheless, large numbers of seminary students are graduating and stepping into leadership positions who have never been exposed in all their three or four years of theological education to any study of prayer dynamics in depth.

For the most part, courses on prayer are considered a harmless hanger-on in theological education. At best, prayer is taken to have some bearing on character or theological formation, or to be a creative expression of belief. It may, on the other hand, be considered unhealthily "otherworldly," or "irrelevant," preventing the Christian from true involvement with the problems of life. In the growing enthusiasm for "holy worldliness," a church member would be made to feel peculiar indeed if he begged off from another discussion group on world affairs in order to have time to pray about world affairs.

In short, from the viewpoint of the average, well-educated, liberal Christian, prayer is definitely not considered to be a vital force. It is not considered to be union with an objective Power. It is thought to be merely a symbolic expression of vital human will and human creativity.

The occasional church member or theological student who has become aware of this "hidden hunger" for a deeper understanding of prayer is left to his own devices. Soon he finds himself floundering in a bewildering morass of literature. Hopefully he tries out a few experiments and disciplines. He has no director. He doesn't know where to turn to find one. Perhaps after a while he joins or tries to organize a feeble prayer group which dies in infancy.

Of course there are many outstanding exceptions to this state of affairs. There are some church leaders who have learned to pray. There are some vital prayer groups that have changed lives. But the average Christian doesn't know where to find them. Probably he doesn't even know they exist.

It is no accident that so many of our young people have turned away from the church feeling that it has little to offer them. It is no accident that so many turn to drugs or mystic cults to help them explore the deeper levels of their being. It is not surprising that so many older members of our churches have not learned to look on the church as the source of beauty, joy, wisdom, refreshment, and power.

It is a tragedy that the Christian church has so little to offer the hungry ones who long to explore deeper into the reality of God than is possible through committees and discussion groups.

But prayer alone is not enough. The problem is deeper than the lack of prayer groups and prayer courses. Our prayer neglect arises from a deeper, more threatening neglect—the neglect of the living Christ.

Prayer existed in the world long before the Christian era. It was a special kind of prayer on which the church was founded, unlike any other kind of praying. It is *prayer through the living Christ* which is the prayer that becomes our joy and strength and uniqueness.

Slowly through the years as theological student, parish

minister, wife and mother, I learned this truth: if prayer is the strength of the Christian, Christ is the strength of prayer. Prayer undertaken by our own unaided, well-meaning efforts usually becomes only one more source of strain in a life already too full of tension.

The prayer with which the first Christians embraced the suffering world was prayer infused with power generated beyond the human dimension. Perhaps we do not need to use that unpopular word "supernatural," but we must somehow make it clear that the prayer which changes lives does not arise from the context of our five senses and the three dimensions. The power which is the living Christ meets our life at its depths. It is "relevant," but it streams from the Christ who was not merely incarnated but is also risen. He lived—yes. But he also *lives*. And he lives in power. On this central fact is grounded the uniqueness which is Christian prayer.

This is not a book on mysticism. That path is the calling of the few. I wrote it for any Christian who wonders whether he is the praying type, and who wonders if prayer, after all, makes any sense or difference in this world. I wrote it first of all for myself, because I asked those questions. I am angry because the churches and seminaries around me had not forestalled those questions by providing bread before I began to suffer with hunger. But I am also grateful, because from those same churches I finally heard voices answering my own with far greater wisdom than my own. We aren't dead yet, we churches, we Christians. Christ has seen to that!

15

I. The Foundations of Christian Prayer

1. "I Am the Vine"

"We confess that we have no answers." I recently heard a young minister preaching. "We are still searching for the truth. The ultimate word of the New Testament is spoken from the cross, when Christ in his pain and desolation and darkness yet remained steadfast in his outpouring of love. That is what Christianity is all about in this uncertain world. We are to love even in the midst of darkness, without requiring or receiving answers."

This sounds beautiful. It is noble, sophisticated, and much in line with the present fashions in theology. *But it is not Christianity!*

What has happened to our Good News? "I came that they may have life, and have it abundantly," said Jesus Christ. But for most of us good, reliable church workers that is still just a promise, a lovely wistful dream. For most of us it has not become a fulfilled reality.

Let us be honest with ourselves. Committee work in the

church isn't much different from committee work any-where. We aren't less worry-ridden, less problem-beset than is our neighbor who hasn't been to church in ten years. Every Sunday the minister blesses us with "the peace of God which passes all understanding," but where is it? We are as tired and anxious as we were before. So we conclude sadly that perhaps God has meant us to work lovingly in the midst of tension and insecurity. Why, after all, should we be given more happiness and answers than other men? Maybe it is more humble to live in the uncertainty and unsatisfied hunger that is all around us. And if we find it difficult, we must try harder.

But this is not Christianity!

We are trying too hard. That sounds strange when churches are urging their members to try harder and harder to meet the challenges of the twentieth century. Never before has the conscience of the churches been so awake and alert to the problems of injustice. Never before have we been so aware of and responsive to the work of scientists and psychologists. Our churches are full of earnest, hardworking committees trying to give one an-other the latest theology, the best of religious education, the most expanded opportunities for loving service. Com-mittees, forums, coffee houses, "buzz sessions," drives, canvasses, counseling services, dinners, workshops, the best of music, the best of sermons, attractive efficient church buildings. We are trying to the point where we feel we can't possibly take on one more committee. And we can be very sure that every year another book will be published

20

pointing out where we have failed and where and how we should try harder.

This is where our great mistake is made. Forgetting about the Resurrection and Pentecost which followed the Cross, forgetting about the Good News and the promised abundant life, we flog ourselves into greater efforts. We try so hard to imitate the love of Christ, at the same time assuring ourselves at the end of every discussion group, every forum: "Of course, no one has any final answers."

Reread the New Testament. We were promised fire, not a feeble flicker. We were promised light, like that of a city set on a hill. We were promised joy. We were promised fulfillment for our hunger. We were promised the radiance of the marriage banquet and a sense of excited discovery like that of a man who finds fantastic treasure buried in a field.

As we read Jesus' words, we begin to realize that somehow we have missed the main point. Christ didn't come to set the example of a noble life and death which we were to imitate. No one could have surpassed Socrates in dying nobly for a cause. Nor did he come merely to tell us to try harder to do justly and love mercy. No one had challenged men better than Amos and Jeremiah and Isaiah. He didn't come to answer philosophical questions or to ask better ones. Plato and Aristotle had already done that. He didn't even come to tell us how to develop mystical experiences. The sophistication and wisdom of the Hindu saints can hardly be surpassed when it comes to mysticism. He didn't even come to tell us to try harder

21

to forgive and love our brothers. That had all been said
centuries earlier by Buddha.

So what did he come for?

He came to bring himself. He came to bring power to
do and be those things that God requires of us. "To all
who received him, . . . he gave power to become children
of God," we are told in the Gospel of John. This can be
said of no other noble martyr or prophet. They gave us
their words and their example, but they could not give us
the power to become like them. Only one has done that.
That is why we call him Savior.

It is his resurrected strength in which we are to stand.
Here is no hero we merely remember. Here is one who has
loved the world and never left it. He is with us now as
much and even more as when he was among us in the
flesh. He invites us to surrender ourselves to the onrush of
his matchless energy. "I am the true vine. . . . Abide in
me, and I in you. . . . You are the branches. He who abides
in me, and I in him, he it is that bears much fruit."
(John 15:1-5.)

Until we have somehow grasped this, we won't make
much progress in our Christian life. This is not a mystical
doctrine. This life of surrender to the living Christ is
possible for all, whether we are the "spiritual type" or not.

There was a certain deacon I knew in a little church
where I was once minister. He was a large, strong man
who ran his business well, though he had had little education. He was kindly and warm and had held the little
church together for a long time by the very force of his

personality. "That little church is the only thing that held on to me when I was a 'dead-end' kid," he used to say briefly. He was not a well-read man and certainly had no subtlety at all. He wouldn't have recognized a mystical experience if it had stared him in the face. He did what he thought to be the right and kind thing every day of his life, but he wouldn't have understood anything about spiritual advancements and illuminations.

What could I preach to such a man? I was a new seminary graduate and full of intricate theology and mystical literature. It used to make me uneasy. What in the world did he and I have in common? The very hymns we sang often worried me, because I kept wondering if they made any sense to him at all: "Teach me some melodious sonnet, sung by flaming tongues above," or "Let all mortal flesh keep silence, and with fear and trembling stand," or "Still, still with thee, when purple morning breaketh."

He sang these hymns in humility and obedience to the minister's strange taste in hymns. But they must have been utterly irrelevant to his life. What could he possibly know about raptures of God-union in purple dawns? He lived in a tiny Chicago apartment with trucks roaring past his door all day long; and he did what he could for his church because he loved it and it had helped him once.

I didn't know what to say to him then. But now I know what would have reached him and strengthened him in the reality of his life, because finally it reached me. I would tell him, meaning every word literally: "That man

23

Jesus we talk about so much in these churches is still alive, you know. His love and his power to do good have not left the world. You know what it is to love and wish to help this church. Well, Jesus Christ feels this even more strongly. He wants to help this church, and he can do it through us—just as a tree wants to produce fruit and does it through the branches. All we have to do is know he is with us, then turn ourselves over to him, asking him to take us as we are and change us as he wishes. We don't have to feel anything, you know. Some people don't feel anything special when they open the door to Christ. But he takes us at our word and starts his work through us that very day."

My deacon would have understood this. This would have met him at the point where he was. He wouldn't have needed to become any other type than what he was already to understand and accept this. He could have laid hold of this central meaning of his church and relied on it in all practical affairs.

He would have understood this better than I understood it for many years, befuddled as I was with much theology. It is hard for ministers and theologians to understand the direct blunt fact at the center of Christianity, that Christ still lives. We mythologize. We allegorize. We idealize. We use words and phrases meaning one thing while our congregations mean another. How very hard it is for us to understand, accept, and build upon the fact that the Christ about whom we talk so much still lives.

There is a prayer written by the Catholic English novelist Evelyn Waugh, in one of his best books, *Helena*, which may well be a prayer for all of us who have found it hard to find God, being much weighed down with the riches of education. Helena, the mother of the Emperor Constantine, newly converted to Christianity, is visiting Bethlehem and meditating upon the three wise men who finally found their way to the infant Christ. She compares their long journey to that of her own, her son, and all who have found their way laboriously to the simplicity of Christ.

"Like me," she said to them, "you were late in coming. The shepherds were here long before; even the cattle. They had joined the chorus of angels before you were on your way. . . . How laboriously you came, taking sights and calculating, where the shepherds had run barefoot! How odd you looked on the road, attended by such outlandish liveries, laden with such preposterous gifts!

"Yet you came, and were not turned away. You too found room before the manger. Your gifts were not needed, but they were accepted . . . for they were brought with love. In that new order of charity that had just come to life, there was room for you too. . . .

"You are my especial patrons . . . and patrons of all latecomers who have a tedious journey to make to the truth, of all who are confused with knowledge and speculation, . . . of all who stand in danger by reason of their talents.

"For His sake who did not reject your curious gifts, pray always for the learned, the oblique, the delicate. Let them

25

not be quite forgotten at the Throne of God when the simple come into their kingdom." [1]

How hard for some of us to find this. What a miracle life becomes when we do! The overwhelming good news is that we don't need to struggle any longer for a perfect vision of God that we have worked out ourselves. We don't need to struggle for the perfect love of the neighbor. We can stand in the force and light of the one personality who had set no barriers whatever against God. We can ask to find God through the eyes of Christ. We can ask to see our brother through the eyes of Christ.

For example, we all know people whom we find almost impossible to love. It seems a hypocrisy even to try, and we are under constant tension when they are around, torn between what we consider our Christian duty and what we actually feel. I remember one elderly couple I visited once in their home. Everything they said, every opinion they expressed was against everything I stood for. They were bigots, racists, and isolationists. Their minds were closed to new ideas. As I talked with them I could almost feel myself shriveling with disgust and irritation. Love them as a Christian? I could hardly bear to sit in the room with them. Suddenly for the first time in my life the thought came to me: "Why, it's not up to *me* to love them. How silly to try to force myself. The living Christ already loves them. He sees beneath their rigid little minds

[1] Evelyn Waugh, *Helena* (Garden City, N.Y.: Doubleday Image Book, 1950).

26

and knows what they've suffered and what wistful dreams they've had. At this very minute his love surrounds them, the way my love surrounds my child. All I have to do is let go, relax, stop pushing myself into feelings I don't have, and ask *him* to take over. I can stop fighting and let him love them through me. What I feel need not matter. What matters is his power that can work through me if I let it."

The immediate release from tension that swept through me is almost indescribable. I still disagreed with all their opinions. They were still unattractive people. But now Christ was carrying the situation. His power, not my feelings, went to work in that room. I couldn't cope, but *he* could. The whole atmosphere of hostility on my part and defensiveness on their part was changed. We disagreed, but the door was no longer closed between us. New creation had become possible again.

Lightness and freedom are offered us, no matter what we have to face that frightens us, angers us, or tempts us. We don't need to clench our teeth and endure it. Christ has faced all these things, overcome them, and still faces them for us. His life in history once for all broke through the walls of unendurable things, impossible things, unconquerable things. His risen life can break through them again for us when we give ourselves to him.

The Christian who knows himself possessed by Christ does not claim to be a better man than his neighbor. He doesn't have a blueprint in his hand for solving all the problems of the world. He claims one thing. He claims that a unique force from the very Source of all life possesses, shapes, and guides him. This force has planted new life in him which in time will change him.

It is not true humility to pretend that this is not a strong, definite, and radiant answer to our basic questions about life. If we claim no part in that strength we may still be good, earnest people, but we have not yet found the heart of Christ.

Christianity was meant to be received with a groan of relief. It was meant to be like hot food after hours of hunger. It was meant to be a consummated marriage after a long betrothal. Expectation and preparation have their own joys, but they are not the same as the joys of fulfillment.

In this uniqueness of Christian relationship, we can explore the uniqueness which is Christian prayer.

2. Prayer and Action

Mary and Martha—a most misunderstood story! Most people are familiar with the story in the tenth chapter of Luke about the two sisters of Lazarus who were hostesses to Jesus on more than one occasion. Mary, at this particular time, sat at Jesus' feet to listen to him. Martha chose to rush around the kitchen, cooking an elaborate meal. Jesus mildly reproved Martha who was trying to get Mary back into the kitchen, telling her that Mary had made the better choice.

Generally it is assumed that Martha was the complete activist, always organizing, always efficiently at work, and that Mary by nature was the dreamer, the spiritual one, the one who sat around imitating the lilies of the field and developing the "higher" side of life.

For all we know it may well have been *Martha* who was the dreamy, the inefficient one, who of course got upset when left alone for once to get a company meal on the table. It was, perhaps, *Mary* who was the natural efficient organizer and leader in the home, who knew when to stop organizing and sit down and listen. She may have been the best cook and housekeeper in Bethany!

Naturally we can't tell at this distance. But unfortunately the image continues in the church down to the present day. Most people still assume that the praying, contemplative Christian is the dreamer, the vague gentle one, the one who can't be trusted to be efficient whether working in the kitchen or on the Every Member Canvass. They are the Marys of the church. Let them talk and pray. They can at least inspire the rest of us!

But then there are the Marthas, so goes the myth. The *doers* of the word. They are much too busy to pray. Let them run the church and the practical affairs of a Christian's life. After all, they are carrying out what the Marys are praying about, aren't they?

A most amusing little incident is told in Albert E. Day's *Autobiography of Prayer:* "In a lifeboat adrift at sea, one strapping fellow frightened by their plight wailed that he was going to pray. A hard-boiled seaman shouted: 'Let the *little* fellow pray. *You* stick to the oars!' "

Quite so. How well we understand that reaction. It is usually our own. In fact, in present-day "religionless Christianity" the so-called praying type of Christian has sunk even lower in the scale and lost whatever doubtful usefulness he had. It now appears that the fellow at the oars, worn out and scared silly, is the one who is *really* praying

30

because he is so actively involved in the situation. Martha, it seems, is the sister who is really contemplating Christ. After all, isn't she the one who is realistically relating to other people's needs?

This is often heard from the modern pulpit and press. The theory is that "to work is to pray." One author expresses it this way: "We do not discover God in prayer and thereafter take him with us into our daily work. . . . It is in the daily work that he reveals himself and gives himself to us. We pray most really when we live most deeply." [1]

Bishop John Robinson writes in a similar vein: "My own experience is that I am really praying for people, . . . precisely *as* I meet them and really give my soul to them. . . . Prayer is the responsibility to meet others with *all* I have." [2]

One hesitates to attack this point of view, because one would seem to imply that he underestimates loving involvement with others. But it must be pointed out that there is more than one way of being lovingly involved.

What do we think Jesus was doing when he withdrew from the crowds for a night of solitary prayer? Why didn't he stay right down there with the hungry, sick multitude, healing them? The usual answer is that he was tired. He needed a time of retreat to be inspired again, so he could

[1] W. B. J. Martin, *The Diary of Peter Parson* (Nashville: Abingdon Press, 1957), p. 106.

[2] John A. T. Robinson, *Honest To God* (Philadelphia: The Westminster Press, 1963), pp. 99-100.

go on and work even better the next day. The implication seems to be that it is a pity that such retreats are necessary. How much better if we were so made that we could stay right on the job. Jesus' experience of ecstasy on the Mount of Transfiguration, from this point of view, seems to be justified because it gave him the energy to go down the mountain and heal the epileptic boy. So many sermons are preached on that theme. "Now don't think you can spend much time in selfish contemplation," we are told in essence. "Don't get lost in prayer (as if there were any danger of that with the average church member!). Remember there are people who need you. Faith without works is dead, you know. Get off that mountain top as soon as you can and get to work. After all, work is the best kind of prayer."

But there is another explanation for Jesus on the mountain top. It *was* work. Another way of working. His body was still. He was not talking to anyone or putting his hands on anyone. He was alone during most of the nights of prayer. Do we think, therefore, that this was a private feast between himself and God, with his wretched brothers forgotten? Not at all. It is more than likely that those hours of private prayer were the most direct, powerful work of healing and reconciliation that he ever did for the world. As he gave himself to the Father through his surrendered prayer, he was *at that moment* releasing the fire and power of the Father into the suffering world. This power of God would, of course, be demonstrated openly the next day as he moved among

32

the crowds; but it would be at work also, that night, in more hidden powerful ways over the whole earth.

Prayer is work! How could it be otherwise? What actually are we doing when we pray? We are moving into the very heart of the Power which controls all power. Who is this God we contact through prayer? The Scriptures describe him in many ways, and all the analogies imply overwhelming energy: fire, wind, warrior, king, bridegroom. God's Kingdom is described by Jesus always in terms of thrusting growth and power: yeast, seed, fermenting wine, vineyards and trees, advancing armies, invested wealth. They used the analogies of energy they had. Perhaps we would use others today. When we touch this God of all being, all energy, growth, change, rapture, can things possibly remain the same within and around us?

What is the praying man doing? "He feeds new energy into the life stream itself into the very atmosphere of living," writes Gerald Heard. "He is in touch with the center of all power. . . . He has touched the mainspring. . . . We are not attaining to a growing aloofness as we climb the three flights of prayer but on the contrary to a growing power, freedom, creativeness, and immediacy." [3]

I believe this is uniquely true through the prayer in Christ. On our own, by our own efforts, we know that our ability to communicate deeply with the Father is far from

[3] Gerald Heard, A *Preface to Prayer* (New York: Harper & Bros., 1944), pp. 158-61.

33

perfect. But when we relate to the Father through his Christ who was completely surrendered, we are related to that surrender. Our ability then to be channels of his love poured into the world is immeasurably increased.

The men and women who have been the most mature and experienced in prayer have not been cloistered personalities unaware of the problems of the world. The mature in prayer best known to me have been a professor of science, an economist, a secretary in a bank, a physician, a school teacher, an astronomer, an actress, a nurse, a housewife, the secretary of a minister. Their lives are overflowing with action and responsibility. They have very little spare time. But their action flows from a center of poise and authority which they know very well is not their own creation. They don't give the appearance of "pious" personalities, and they don't even talk very much about prayer unless asked. They are very human. But they know they are not acting alone.

Without exception they believe that their time of prayer is the most effective of all their actions. They believe that their lives and the lives around them are being changed as much during the moments of surrendered prayer as during the moments of more obvious external work. Their times of prayer are in no sense a retreat. They are an advance. They are not merely being inspired. Through the resurrected strength of Christ they are changing the world.

We have already known this to be true in the lives of the giants of both prayer and action: Paul, Augustine,

Bernard of Clairvaux, Francis of Assisi, Joan of Arc, Theresa of Avila, John of the Cross, Thomas Aquinas, Catherine of Siena, Martin Luther, George Fox, John Wesley. They were politicians, warriors, reformers, authors, teachers, organizers. Who can separate them into the categories of Marthas of action and Marys of prayer? Not only did their action flow from their prayer, but they knew their prayer was the supreme kind of action. It was true for them. It can be equally true for us.

Seemingly impossible things were demanded of the church by Christ: to heal the sick, to raise the dead, to reconcile the hostile, to cast out the demonic that preys on our lives. We try so pathetically to make ourselves over into men and women of such power. But we can't do it. We were never meant to do it. We were asked one thing: to join ourselves to the unconquerable life which is the risen Christ. And the works he demands of us will be fulfilled through the prayer which is in his name.

Therefore the Christian need never apologize for the time he firmly sets aside for this special kind of work. He is helping his brother, his neighborhood, his church, his family, and the suffering world as much during those quiet minutes as when he is talking to them or physically working for them.

What a joy it would be for the disabled Christian to realize this. Often the old and the ill feel so useless. But they can still actively share in the work of the world as they read the newspaper, listen to the radio, observe people's faces. As the Christian meditates over snatches of conversation, problems of friends, news items which have aroused his compassion, he can bring them into the light of Christ and commit people and their concerns trustingly to that healing light. And by that act of commitment Christ's risen energy is poured into the situation. By his act of surrendered prayer the world is a little better than it was before. Sometimes he will see the results almost immediately. Sometimes he won't see them for a long time. Perhaps never. But he will know with increasing assurance that God has used his prayer as a means to help the world in some way that it needed helping.

Once, in church, I saw a woman I knew fairly well in the pew behind me. Her face looked tired and tense. I didn't know what her problem was, but I found myself praying that the light of Christ would surround her and that his peace that passes understanding would come to her. Several times during the service I found myself again praying silently for her peace. After the service we walked out together. "I was so upset when I came to the service today," she told me quietly. "It's a rather complicated problem and I can't explain it all now, but during the service I found myself thinking over and over the words 'The peace of God, the peace of God.' And it became real to me. I do feel peaceful now." We had not talked together. She did not know of my prayer for her. But God was able to take the offered love and trust in his power and do with it some important work in her heart.

Usually we do not see such quick results. Many times I have seen a certain expression on the face of some person

36

passing me in the street, and for years afterward I have felt impelled to pray for that person, though he was utterly unknown to me. I will never know the results of those prayers for passing strangers, but I know those prayers are not wasted. They are one way of working in God's Kingdom, and God uses these prayers according to his will.

3. Prayer and Mysticism

At the theological seminary where I was a student, a small group of us thought quite sincerely that to be interested in prayer was to be interested in mysticism. We developed quite a little cult. I shall never forget the expression on the face of one of the elderly ministers who, during alumni week, had stepped innocently in one of the students' rooms which he himself had occupied many years earlier. "It was almost completely dark," he reported later. "There was a piece of black velvet on the wall with a votive light flickering in front of it. And there was a huge picture on the velvet—no, not Jesus. It was one of those half-dressed Hindu saints in a trance or something. What are they *teaching* them in seminary these days?"

Our professors were, in fact, completely blameless. Perhaps too blameless. We were hungry for something and thought mystical disciplines might be the answer. We experimented completely on our own, and, as is to be expected, within a few months we were quite fed up and worn out with our fruitless efforts.

I learned then that if mysticism were the Good News of Christianity it would never save the world. Only very few are called to the path of mystical experience, and even fewer can sustain it.

Jesus was the one great mystic who did not teach mysticism. Obviously he knew all there was to know about the experience of absolute union with the Source of all being. There are hints of it in the New Testament:

And when he came up out of the water, immediately he saw the heavens opened and the Spirit descending upon him like a dove; and a voice came from heaven, "Thou art my beloved Son." (Mark 1:10-11.)

And as he was praying, the appearance of his countenance was altered, and his raiment became dazzling white. (Luke 9:29.)

But in spite of these tantalizing glimpses very little is said by either Jesus or his disciples about the mystical experience of cosmic consciousness. When asked by his disciples to teach them to pray, he taught them an astonishingly matter-of-fact way of praying which we call the Lord's Prayer. It is not a prayer for a mystic. It is the kind of prayer that can be prayed by any ordinary Christian who trusts the Father. It deals not with states of purgation, awakening, and illumination, but with the ordinary concerns of any Christian as he relates to God and his brother: reverence, obedience, the petition for physical help, forgiveness, the request for guidance and protection.

It is almost as if Jesus took the mystical experience for granted, at least for himself. He seemed to feel he was in the world for another purpose altogether. He knew that if the healing of the world depended on the achievement of mystical experience, the large majority of the world would remain unredeemed.

It was the New Creation for which he came. The rebirth. The new direction. The kingdom of God, which is the coming of his life and his will into the lives of men. Anybody, whether called to the mystical path or not, may turn at any moment to the Christ and pray: "Take me into your light of resurrection. Change me. I am given over to you now and wish you to work your will through me." And that person, no matter who he is or what his temperament, will be possessed and changed into a new being. And through Christ he will be changed as swiftly and completely as if he had spent years struggling up the mountain of mystical sanctity.

I knew a woman once, charming, beautiful, well educated, but quite a lightweight when it came to serious reading and thinking. She believed in God in a conventional way. I doubt if she prayed outside of church. She certainly never showed any mystical tendencies whatever, or any signs of great moral muscle. Her family concluded she was their lovely butterfly, their charming Peter Pan. Not much was expected of her. Her life took a sudden

tragic turn, and she made a series of extremely serious
mistakes which threatened for a while to spoil her own
life and those she most loved. As the horror of self-
knowledge grew on her and she saw where her life had
led her, she stood alone in her room one day, and simply
gave herself over to God. She knew she had spoiled her
life for herself, and whatever life remained to her was
from that moment on to be in the hands of Christ.
Whatever he wanted her to do or be was dependent on
his will and work in her. Many years have passed since
then. She remains charming and beautiful. Her extremely
busy and efficient life allows little time for heavy reading
or long prayer disciplines. Nor has she the temperament
for them. But she has become the most mature in faith
and prayer of any person I have known. Many turn to her
for healing, consolation, and strength. And though she is
often tired and faces many problems, there is an inner
joy and serenity which is unmistakable and triumphant.
She never has been and never will be the "mystical type."
She is something far more important—a new creation in
Christ.

This power of Christ can lay hold of any man or woman
in this way, no matter what his temperament or what his
problem. And though few are the mystical type, everyone is the praying type if the prayer is through Christ. The
Christian can be joyfully relaxed when he prays. He need
not and must not strive for sensations and emotions. That
is what we would-be mystics at our theological seminary
did not realize. We strove for many disciplines. We

examined every sensation under a spiritual microscope. We were utterly without humor and extremely tense about it. It never occurred to us that to belong to Christ is utter freedom and gaiety of heart. "He that loves, flies, runs, and rejoices; he is free and not bound," we are told in Thomas à Kempis' *Imitation of Christ*. It never occurred to us that the mystical calling in Christ is a gift, not an attainment; that the true mystic is not grim about it but gay about it; that every Christian can be gay in his prayers whether mystic or not, because he belongs to Christ and through him to the Eternal Being. What he needs will be given, and it will be what *he* needs. And it will be given according to *his* capacity. Nothing will be forced on him which he is not ready to take, and nothing will be withheld from him which he is ready to take. He is in the safest, wisest hands in the universe. Through eternity there will be all the time needed for the perfect mystical vision of God's heart to unfold to us. But in Christ we are already at that heart of being, by faith if not by sight.

We are to ask simply for the gift of the Holy Spirit. He will give us the gift which we can best receive. It may be teaching, or healing, or leadership. It may be a power of intercession, or the ability to read hearts and counsel and guide. And of course, it *might* be the mystical experience.

If God calls us to that life of mysticism, we will feel the deepening hunger for it. There is no need to grab for it greedily or turn away in fear. If it is genuine it will not manifest itself as a coarse compulsion making us oblivious to the world around us. It is a sure sign of unhealthy escapism or neurosis if we become selfish or proud. To the genuine mystic, life does not become vague or unimportant. On the contrary, the life around him becomes more sharply distinct and increasingly significant in a new way. The church has badly neglected the occasional genuine mystic in its fellowship. Seldom is understanding given or healthy, experienced leadership offered to the person who is granted this gift. His is usually a lonely path, and usually he must depend on his books and the personal guidance he receives through his praying.

It is a great and blessed gift and offers much good to the world. But it is not better or more precious in God's sight than other gifts. One whose vocation is mysticism is not any closer to God simply because he can *feel* that closeness. Nor is the mystic excused from compassionate concern with the world's problems. For the Christian, the mystical experience must be within the context of the rebirth in Christ, accepted as one of the many gifts of his friendship.

4. But
Is It So?

But after all, is it really so? How do we really know we are not deluding ourselves with all this emphasis on union with Christ? It is so easy to imagine things. How easily we project on the universe the image of our own wishful thinking. Someone might say there is a purple cow in that corner of the room, to which he is drawn for strength. And who can prove him wrong or right?

Some ancient mystery cults taught that their gods, for example Mithras and Osiris, risen and triumphing, were in union with their believers. Who believes in them now? After all, isn't perhaps this Christian sacramental bit just another enlarged mystery cult based on imagination, superstition, and psychological need? . . .

Thus our thinking might travel in our painfully honest and inquiring moments. Perhaps we might question ourselves further, as we think about prayer:

Perhaps prayer is just a kind of self-hypnosis which may

have creative or destructive results according to our healthy adjustment to life and other people. What possible evidence is there that prayer is really connected with some objective reality which changes us?

So we call ourselves branches connected to the vine of Christ. What if there is no actual vine "out there," but just the vine of our common humanity? Why not define prayer as the acceptance of our oneness with humanity and as such consider it a good thing? How do we know that Christ is really risen or really exists? Are we deluded? Superstitious? Childish? . . .

There are, to be sure, many Christians who do not ask themselves these questions and do not seem to feel the need of evidence. This discussion is not for them, except insofar as they may be concerned to give reasons to others for the faith they profess. But there are many Christians who long for some reasonable evidence other than the fact that they *feel* it to be so.

These inquirers and analyzers find it painfully inadequate to be told: "Evidence is not necessary. You must make the leap of faith by decision. It does not matter if a thing is objectively true, so long as you decide for yourself that for you it *shall* be true."

It is equally frustrating to be told: "Evidence is useless, because even facts, if known, will not induce people to have faith. Besides, if people believe because of facts rather than trust alone, they may have selfish motives!"

Every serious inquirer has had these answers given to him in all possible forms and variations. Unfortunately,

45

though they are sincerely meant, they give the impression of dodging and sidestepping. Of course one must sooner or later make the decision for faith, but is this faith to be based on no evidence at all? To be sure, the demonstration of facts cannot force people into faith, but evidence can and does provide a healthy basis for rethinking one's faith or lack of it. A lover marries primarily because of his love and trust, but sooner or later somewhere along the line he must face the actual question: "What kind of woman is she anyway—aside from the fact that I love her?" In these days when we understand so much more about the power of the subconscious to rationalize, invent, defend, and project, we will do well to inquire concerning the facts underlying our beliefs.

Did Christ actually rise from the dead? Or do we mean merely that his disciples' love and faith arose from the dead? Is Christ actually alive now? When we say he is alive, do we mean that he is self-aware and responsive to us? Or do we merely mean that his influence and the memory of him are alive in his church? Can we actually communicate with him, knowing he hears and responds in at least as real a way as our friends hear and respond?

Many schools of theology today teach that the literal belief in the now living Christ as an objective reality is a childish crudity that the church should have outgrown. It is the Christ influence risen in the hearts of his followers that matters, they insist. Our prayers to him raise our faith. No supernatural strength flows through the sacraments of Baptism or Communion. These are symbols through which the corporate faith of the church community acts on us. Perhaps the same words are used in the church service that at one time referred to supernatural reality, but all thinking persons realize that these concepts are symbols or mythological expressions. When the living Christ is mentioned or when we pray in his name, we don't mean anything "out there" which calls itself the Christ. We mean the way of life he brought, in which a man lives for others. Thus many theologians and church leaders reason today.

The average church member should know this—often he does not—so he can ask his teachers and ministers what they really mean by the words they use. Let us admit at the outset that even our best words are symbolic. All language is symbolic, based on images which refer to aspects of our environment. A tree, for example, can be seen and interpreted in many different ways. A physicist may think of the tree as a form of energy with a certain molecular structure. A biologist will see a tree as a certain form of vegetable life with its own form of assimilation and reproduction. A gardener will see a tree as an aspect of his landscaping, with concern for its nutritional needs, its foliage, its decorative qualities. A child will see a tree as a thing of beauty, mystery, or adventure. If we had more than five senses, a tree would seem, perhaps, as different from what we see now as the caterpillar's vision of a tree is different from ours. And though a tree may appear the same to ordinary people looking at it, who can prove that everyone sees what we call green and brown

47

(also symbols) in the same way? Also, the tree will appear one way at night, another way at high noon. In the mist it will be one thing and in the snow quite another. A stunted dwarf pine as well as a giant redwood are called by the name of tree, though they seem so widely different.

The word "tree" is a symbol referring to a certain reality in our environment. And this symbol must cover many varieties and interpretations. The use of this word "symbol" is a convenient shortcut in ordinary conversation, but when those seriously interested in the subject talk together it is well to know in what way, according to what interpretation, this word is being used. It would be particularly important to define terms and symbols if a psychologist and a philosopher were in the group: one might be thinking of a tree as a delusion rising from the subconscious; the other might be thinking of it as a form without reality in itself, real only insofar as it is perceived by someone's mind. At this point the question would have to be asked: Does this symbolic term "tree" refer to a reality which has objective existence apart from us? Or does it refer to a collective state of mind which takes this form?

Granted that the words God, Christ, resurrection, eternal life are all symbols; granted the symbol can never cover or adequately describe the reality to which it refers; nevertheless it can be made clear whether there *is* a reality to which the speaker is referring. It can and should be made clear if the reality referred to exists in and of itself. If the speaker is using a symbolic term such as "the

48

living Christ" with one thing in mind while the majority of his listeners have quite another concept in mind, a state of confusion and semihypocrisy results which is fairly typical of our churches today.

I suggest that the next time we hear the symbolic phrase "the living Christ," we ask such pointed questions as: What do you mean by living? Actually alive, knowing he is alive, alive at least as far as I am myself with conscious awareness and response? What do you mean by Christ? A memory in the mind of God and man? A power that enters our lives and changes them? And is this *his* power, independent of our existence? Or is this power merely the force of our combined faith? The answers (if we are fortunate enough to get a direct answer at all) will be interesting and perhaps surprising.

The church should know what it is talking about when it speaks of "the living Christ." I submit it makes a profound difference whether we are talking of a Christ risen in his own independent being, or a Christ risen merely in the memory of his church. It would, we agree, make more than a slight difference whether we ourselves exist in our own right, or only as a subjective impression of our combined relatives and friends. A person is either alive or he isn't.

Is Christ alive? On what basis can we form an opinion? On what grounds can we choose to give the gift of ourselves in faith?

There is, of course, no proof as a scientist would understand the word. At least not yet. But there is a vast amount of evidence that might bring us to the point where we no longer have reasonable doubt. There are two kinds of evidence. The first of these is the evidence of the documents written in the early years of the church. The first reference to the resurrected Christ appears in Paul's letters to the Thessalonians and Corinthians, written perhaps eighteen or twenty years after the death of Jesus.

We would not have you ignorant, brethren, concerning those who are asleep, that you may not grieve as others do who have no hope. For since we believe that Jesus died and rose again, even so, through Jesus, God will bring with him those who have fallen asleep. (I Thess. 4:13-14.)

He was buried, . . . he was raised on the third day. . . . Then he appeared to more than five hundred brethren at one time, most of whom are still alive. . . . Then he appeared to James, then to all the apostles. Last of all, as to one untimely born, he appeared also to me. (I Cor. 15:4-8.)

These letters are written as first-hand memory and witness to an overwhelming event in the life of Paul, an educated man of great intelligence, who had formerly been a persecutor of the Christian church. Paul states that he saw the risen Christ himself. Likewise, he refers to other living witnesses who saw the resurrected Jesus.

But even before these letters of Paul were written, the resurrection was taught in the Christian communities as a fact. New Testament scholars agree that there were many detailed narratives of Jesus' life, death, teachings, and resurrection in circulation among the Christian communities from the earliest days of the church. Whether they were in written or verbal form is not known. The four Gospels in their present form, written much later, were largely based on those early accounts of eyewitnesses.

It is often brought forward as evidence of the resurrection that the church leaped to life in spite of the fact that the disciples were frightened, scattered, and in hiding after the crucifixion. It is indeed strange that those disillusioned cowed men were found a few weeks later preaching openly in the streets, almost intoxicated with joy. There is no doubt that they were certain that Jesus was risen, and that his rising was a surprise to them. Their conviction carried them through many years of hard work, travel, physical and emotional strain of every kind, persecution and martyrdom at the end.

Through the centuries, there is also the witness, perhaps not very meaningful or convincing to some of us, of educated, intelligent men and women who have claimed not only to have felt the presence of the risen Lord but also to have seen him. Personally I find it hard to believe that they were all misled by projected images of their own subconscious needs.

There is another kind of evidence, of a different sort entirely, which has become increasingly significant during the past eighty years. The study of parapsychology and psychical research, now slowly gaining reputation in many universities, has accumulated enough experimental material to have overwhelming implications for psychology, philosophy, and theology.

Many scientists approach this subject with suspicion, caution, and even distaste. Nevertheless the carefully documented experiments and observations of such well-known scientists and psychologists as Frederick Myers, Oliver Lodge, William James, Carl Jung, G. N. M. Tyrrell, Gardner Murphy, J. B. Rhine, C. D. Broad cannot be ignored.

Unfortunately many educated and otherwise broad-minded people form negative opinions about the subject of extrasensory perception based on one or two experiences or one or two books they may have read. But those who are open-minded enough to study the official Proceedings of the Society of Psychical Research, or the results of thirty years of experiment by Dr. J. B. Rhine of Duke University, will find abundant evidence that there is far more to the nature of man than can be measured by the five senses or the three dimensions.

In his book *The Reach of the Mind*, Dr. Rhine cautiously concludes:

We have found that there is a capacity for acquiring knowledge that transcends the sensory functions. . . . We now know, too, that space and time do not affect this process as they do phenomena known to be physical; hence it seems that in ESP activity the mind . . . does not depend upon any kind of physical principle known or likely to be derived from the space-time physics of the present day.

He goes on to discuss the relationship of this evidence to the question of survival after death:

If logic alone could be trusted, the evidence of ESP would go far to establish the survival hypothesis on logical grounds. As will be recalled, when ESP was found to function without limitation from time and space, this discovery was taken to mean that the mind is capable of action independent to some degree of the space-time system of nature. Now, all that immortality means is freedom from the effects of space and time; death seems to be purely a matter of coming to a halt in the space-time universe. Therefore the conclusion that there is at least some sort of technical survival would seem to follow as a logical derivation from the ESP research.[1]

This is not proof, of course, as Dr. Rhine is the first to point out. Perhaps there will never be proof. But it is evidence strong enough to enable the serious inquirer to turn with greater interest and confidence to the radiant witness of the apostles and the scores of Christians since, who have claimed to have seen the risen Lord in his transfigured body of light. From this point of view, the Scriptures jump to life in a new and startling way. What we had thought were merely beautiful myths may, after all, be reality!

The risen Christ is no myth. He is still himself, compassionate, powerful, with us forever. If any person ever lived beyond the grave, he is that person. And with excellent evidence that we do in fact survive death, we may all the more be sure that he is the risen, transfigured Lord over us, beyond us, close to us, but independent of us.

The liberal Protestant usually thinks of the Com-

[1] (Clifton, N.J.: Apollo Editions, 1961), pp. 204, 213.

munion service as a memorial alone. For years I interpreted it as such, and it was beautiful but not especially helpful. When I began to realize that Christ is alive and his invisible energy a reality which enfolds us, I learned to think of the Communion service as a genuine sacrament, as one of the means by which the power of his body of light streams into our lives and changes them. We are joined to his healing power, his sacrifice, his resurrection as literally as a branch is joined to its vine.

5. Prayer and Self-deception

Years ago when we visited Geneva, we found a small stone monument half hidden in the bushes along one of the avenues. I do not remember the date it was raised, but I do remember it was put there by the Calvinist Church of Geneva in sorrow and expiation for the persecution and execution of Michael Servetus, burned alive in 1553 for his theological disagreements with John Calvin. The inscription referred sadly to the faulty thinking of those times which could lead good men to persecute one another in the name of Christ.

As we stood looking at this small dark stone, it seemed to grow into a large question mark. It stands for the knottiest question in all the problems about prayer. How can we be sure we are, in fact, being guided by Christ and not our own prejudices and interpretations? John Calvin was a man of prayer and claimed the guidance of Christ. How then could he be so misled by the faulty thinking of his times? Torquemada called on Christ every day of his life and yet condemned heretics to torture and death. Where is the boasted protection from serious error to be found in them and those like them? Where is Christ's guidance? Has the reality of the risen Christ broken through to them? And if so, what went wrong?

There are perhaps two major reasons for self-deception in prayer. The first is the situation in which a *cultural* interpretation of Christ is so overwhelmingly taught that it is almost impossible for the Christian not to identify the real Christ with the prevailing *idea* about Christ. The typical inquisitor, for example, was so firmly convinced that the voice of his church was the voice of Christ, that any dissenting movement was dismissed out of hand as a temptation of Satan. The English or American slave owner of the eighteenth century often was a devout church member and would see no incongruity between his business and the guidance through prayer he felt he received from Christ. To him as to many, Christ's voice was the voice of the established order of his church.

Many examples can be found in our own time, both obvious and subtle. The extreme cases would be certain sects in various parts of America in which the voice of the Christ is firmly believed to be the voice of a Caucasian Protestant. In radical circles, the voice of Christ is that of a protestor against the social order, a revolutionary. More subtle examples are found in our own ordinary, reasonably liberal, middle-of-the-road churches, in which Christ is presented as a sound twentieth-century moderate, with

56

healthy ideas about a well-balanced, comfortable life with lots of friends and a flourishing business and a decent amount of patriotism. It is only too easy to see in Christ what we wish to see, to categorize him according to our own comfort and expectations. It does not occur to the self-deceived to separate Christ from his system. And yet, the Christ we see in the Scriptures was, above all, unpredictable. People could not categorize him, though many tried to even in his own time. He was always breaking through the barriers of the systems raised up around him, making the surprising unforeseen demand and asking the unexpected question. One of the surest signs of the living Christ in our lives is the surprise element. We are led to grow in unexpected ways. The gifts developed within us are not those we had thought were our "type." Sometimes we are led to break with the expectations of those around us, sometimes we are led to conform, but almost always in ways we had not expected. We are made to look at ourselves in new ways and question our accepted values and assumptions, whether radical, conservative, or "middle of the road".

How can we best protect ourselves against this kind of self-deception? The best protection is to realize the constant danger. We must keep alert to the ease with which we identify the living Lord with this movement or that cause or this party or that race. Think how we usually visualize him—a tall, stalwart man with curly brown hair and beard and wistful blue eyes, clothed in a spotless white robe. In all seriousness an objection was recently

57

raised by a devout Christian against a certain illustration in the Church School curriculum books, "because the picture made Jesus look so Jewish"! Yet this is only a visual idolatry, unimportant compared to that of equating the risen Christ with this or that system of thought which happens to be fashionable in our culture.

To be sure, as Christians involved with the problems of the world, we must engage ourselves with systems, ideas, parties, projects. Christ's spirit may indeed be working through these channels. But he is never to be identified with any one organization or system, because at any moment that system or organization may depart from his spirit and sin against him. His risen spirit works through, but is independent of, systems and groups and causes. He is found at work in the most surprising places.

Incidentally, theologians are often the worst offenders. As new trends in theological systems rise and fall, their interpreters are strangely heard in one decade announcing the total weakness of man and man's dependence on the power and the grace and the Word of the transcendent God; and in another decade proclaiming religionless Christianity in which man, now come of age, has found in his freedom and maturity an independence from supernatural projections. Christ is solemnly identified with each new system as it comes along.

There is another safeguard, the living Christ himself. The main theme of this book is that the risen Christ actually does exist in his own independent reality, regardless of what we do or do not think about him. Based on this reality is the conviction that he will break through our self-deceptions, if we are aware of them, and pray to his independent existence. We need not be helpless victims of the cultural interpretations of our Lord.

However, there is a second, more insidious type of self-deception which often creeps upon a person when he is most proudly free of a cultural idol. It is the tendency to worship his *idea* of God rather than God himself. It is the tendency to trust the power of prayer, rather then the power of Christ through the prayer. It is the tendency to trust the Christ as we have spoken of him and prayed to him in the past, rather than the Christ who lives and heals and redeems at the present moment. This creeping corruption in our spiritual lives is very hard to discern. We must remind ourselves that nothing matters, nothing truly lives for us except the living Christ. We cannot trust the prayer or the grace of the past, though we can remember it gratefully. We can only trust and lean on the prayer and grace of the present. Continually we must, in our prayer, throw ourselves upon the Christ of this hour. Each day we can again address him: "I commit myself to you as *you* know yourself to be. My thoughts are often unfree and tied to my desires, memories, expectations. But *you* in your risen light are free. I commit myself to your reality."

But doesn't this divorce us from the safeguarding validity of the Scriptures which, after all, are a record of the past? For the Christian who claims the reality of the living Christ, there is no dichotomy here. The risen Christ

59

is the same as he who lived and died in Palestine. He *is* that Jesus who arose from the dead and dwells in the strength of the Father, ever compassionate. The Scriptures are the foundation of our knowledge of him, and the foundation of our decision to trust him. In many questionable situations they are the touchstone for the settling of belief and conduct. There are times when we must know what Christ actually said about God, our attitude toward others, the signs of the Kingdom, the identifying signs of his true followers, the promises of reward and suffering and their nature. To look to the Scriptures in times of uncertainty is not like looking to the past. Rather, it is to remind ourselves of the concrete reality of that person Jesus and the actualities of his character. The myths of Osiris, Mithras, and other legendary saviors could easily be molded to fit the wishes and needs and special situations of their devotees, for there was no way of checking up by a historical flesh-and-blood record what these saviors (if they had existed at all) actually said and did in specific situations. It is helpful to know, however we may choose to deal with it in these days of "situational ethics," that Jesus actually *did* (for all his compassion) condemn adultery. It may be a good thing to remind ourselves that he *did* say that the possession of great wealth was an extremely dangerous thing and that few people could be reborn spiritually when burdened with wealth. It is advisable to remind ourselves through Scripture that Jesus *did* say that serving another person, whoever he was in whatever situation, was the same as serving him. It is well to be reminded that he believed marriage was a binding tie and that divorce had come into the world because of the "hardness of hearts." It is well to remember that he healed bodies as well as relationships; that he never told anybody that illness was the will of God for them; and that he told his disciples they could through him do greater things than he had done. In short, it is healthy to be reminded of many things about him pictured in the Scriptures which do not conform to our own special brand of theology or our own needs and wishes of the moment. In the Scriptures we are brought up against the Christ who loves us, heals us, but does not conform neatly to our pattern of life. And it is the same with that Christ who is now risen. Triumphant, transfigured, mediating the full strength of the Father, changed into his glorious body now, but still the startling, real Jesus who walked in Palestine. The same spirit. The same savior.

The Scriptures are, thus, a firm rock beneath our vague wavering, conforming, rationalizing selves. If we find ourselves radically departing from the convictions and reality of that historical witness, we can be reasonably sure that we deceive ourselves in our claims to divine guidance.

There are other safeguards and signposts. Are the fruits of the spirit slowly growing, the fruits of compassion, patience, peace, forgiveness, joy, healing of relationships? Are we aware of our freedom to say "no" to the spirit that possesses us, or are we compelled and driven against our real will? Do barriers between us and others seem to be growing or diminishing? Is the world and the life around us becoming more vague, unimportant, and meaningless, or more sharply defined, more exciting, more significant? Are we deliberately turning our backs on known facts? Are doors opening and opportunities for growth arising? Honest answers can provide us with many clues about the genuineness of our claim that Christ guides us.

But even when the fruits of the spirit are coming forth, we may well be in danger of turning our attention to the fruits themselves, trusting them rather than the vine, the giver of the fruits. The supreme safeguard is Christ at this moment, in his unexpectedness, his hiddenness, and his compassion, given to us and yet free of us. To this Christ we are to be obedient.

6. Grace
and Method

The worst thing to say to a child is: "If you do that, mama won't love you any more!" A child should never be made to feel he is earning his parents' love or that there is anything he could do which might kill that love. Many people have been made to feel this way by their parents, and all their lives they feel they are walking on quicksand. What can they count on to be strong and enduring and absolutely secure if their parents' love, the first love to form their infant consciousness, has not been secure?

Likewise the worst thing that can be taught in any religion is a conditional love of God. It is astonishing to see how many people seem to think that God will love them according to their deserts. The central meaning of Christianity is that God meets us, loves us, and helps us as we are. We don't have to earn that love. There is much growing to be done, but this growing is done in the context of love already given. Not only is this love shown in the life of Christ, but our ability to receive and radiate this love is made possible to us by his continuing presence and power.

Why, then, is there any need of method or discipline in prayer? If God, the Father, is personal and understands and loves us as persons, why must there be special times and preparations for this deep relationship of prayer?

The fact is that most of us do not feel God's closeness most of the time. We have evidences of his closeness through growth of courage, understanding, healing of body, or relationships. Sometimes we find that the sign and assurance of his presence is simply our doing steadfastly what we ought to do, with no elation, no inner bugles blowing, just somehow doing what we had thought we couldn't. Occasionally he leads us to the banqueting hall and we are given the gift of riotous joy and delight in the conscious awareness of God. But this is seldom. We walk by faith based on reasonable evidences united with trust, and the sober reality of the growing fruits are the only things permitted to our sight.

It is true that our relation to God, our Source, through Christ, our friend, is a relationship of freely given love. But God works his loving will through an orderly dependable process that we call law. Even Jesus' works of healing were not the breaking of natural law. They were the expression of a profounder law which we can only dimly see and cannot measure at this stage of our development. Think of the works of healing done by a medical missionary among isolated primitive people. The healing he can do on children's diseased eyes, a man's infected foot, or a woman dying in childbirth would seem like fantastic miracles to that primitive group. But the physician knows that he has merely entered more deeply into the secrets of natural law than they have. He understands the world better. He uses drugs and techniques developed through deeper observation and understanding. It is natural to him, though not to them.

Perhaps God's work through our prayer is much the same. Prayer is not merely conversation with God. It is not pleading with him for something which he might not otherwise give. It is not the mere enjoyment of mystical feelings. Prayer is the entering into God's law at the deepest possible level.

The word "law" is a stumbling block to many people. It seems to imply not the personal response of a loving Father but the impersonal reaction of an X-ray machine when we push the right button. Are we actually implying here that God grants prayer according to the technical method we use? Are we implying that God will withold his help to a burned child whose parents are praying hysterically or perhaps not praying at all, while he grants healing to another child whose parents have studied and practiced all the right techniques? Doesn't that turn the universe into a vast machine rather than the Kingdom of our Father?

These are serious questions. They arise very soon, not only when we consider the questions of petition and intercession, but when we consider the whole realm of disciplined prayer. Why are all these formal categories of confession, commitment, adoration, examination of conscience, special times and places necessary at all? Why so legalistic? Where is the loving Father in this whole matter of law, discipline, and method?

Perhaps the whole problem of discipline in prayer can be compared to the problem of sexual method and discipline in a happy marriage. A good marriage is based primarily on mutual trust and honor and self-giving. It *can* remain a loving, trustful marriage without much knowledge of sexual psychology. In some cases the knowledge seems instinctive. In other cases, mistakes are forgiven and healed because of the great love between the pair. But in most marriages some disciplined education of the laws of body, mind, and emotions is needed for the fullest expression and experience of the love that is already there. We meet the marriage partner more completely in his wholeness if we understand something of the structure of his being. Nothing is worse, of course, than a marriage which is nothing but expert technique. That is not marriage but merely mechanics. On the other hand, even a union of deep love and respect can be unenthralling and uncreative without some knowledge of method.

God loves us and accepts us whether we ever learn disciplined prayer or not. He helps us to the extent which we permit him. But how much more forcefully and fully he can show forth his love for us if we have some understanding of the profound laws of prayer. How much more swiftly and completely he can help us.

Perhaps "law" is not the best word in this context. When it is used with reference to God, it means the dependable, impartial quality of his love. He is not haphazard or whimsical. His love has built into the very structure of the universe the answers to all our needs. We who are a part of this universe must learn to cooperate with this structure, organized by his love for our growth. His good will surges everlastingly through all the universe. It is deep, regular, dependable. Prayer is learning to recognize and respond to this limitless dependable goodness.

But why do the answers to our needs seem so hidden? Why don't we find them more easily? We do not know. The potentiality of penicillin existed in the universe for centuries before men discovered it. But in the meantime millions died of infection. Why are God's answers so deeply buried? It has something to do with our growth in the world. It has something to do with our free will. It has something to do with the extent of our truly passionate concern and disciplined dedication to search and discovery.

God's law is not the negation of his love. It is the regular channeling of his love. It does not imply a machine. It implies an orderly working out of creation into our human lives. When we say that prayer is part of the spiritual law, we certainly don't mean that our relationship with the Father is mechanical or impersonal.

Rather, we mean that in our relationship we are permitted more than just talking things over with him.

How exciting if prayer really puts tools in our hands to work with! How changed our whole approach to prayer if it enables us to share in God's very acts of creation among the men and women of this world!

Recently I received a letter from a friend, a university professor of microbiology, who is a believer and leader in prayer. He writes:

We bring all our petitions for both material and spiritual things into our Father's power—for it is our Father's world, . . . the power of God is all around us at all times—just like radio waves—and we have to "tune in" to receive its benefit. . . . Of course, "tuning in" means to be as close to God as possible. This, I believe, is the interpretation of "whatsoever you shall *ask in my Name*, it shall be given you." In my Name, meaning "in my Way," or "in my Spirit." . . . This demands a degree of discipline, of emptying of self, of being prepared to be simply an instrument in his Hand. . . . It demands a complete yielding of body and soul to be used as God directs.

I believe this scientist has put his finger on the central reason for discipline and method in prayer. It teaches us how to surrender—how to let go. It teaches us how to relax the body, the will, the intellect, and the emotions, and to turn these relaxed faculties over to a Power which is not ours. God can only work through us in a very limited way if he must work through our unrelaxed, unsurrendered, tightened-up selves.

My three-year-old daughter once got a bad splinter in her finger. I wanted to help her. I wanted to remove it. But when I got the tweezers and washcloth and sat beside her and tried to take her hand, she clenched her hands into tight fists and began to scream. She was making so much noise that she couldn't even hear my voice trying to soothe her and explain the procedure to her. Her fingers were squeezed so tightly and the muscles so tense that I could not take away the very thing that was hurting her.

This is exactly what often happens when we pray to God. We call for help but are so tense and distrustful that he can't get through to us to help us. The discipline of prayer teaches us how to let God do the thing we are asking of him. It teaches us how to say "yes" to God as he takes us into his hands to heal us and remake us.

To say "yes" to God is the only thing we *can* do for him. All else he does for us. He gives us the health, the love, the strength and wisdom. We stand utterly in his life and power. But the choice whether or not to say "yes" arises from the choice of our own free will, and no one else in all creation can say it for us. Nor can any power in all creation stop us from saying "no" if we choose, and from wandering off into the bewildering darkness of our own fragmented will and being.

Some fortunate people know instinctively how to say "yes" to God's power, but most of us do not. We have to learn how, and the learning is helped and guided by his presence. Every "yes" we say to God when meeting the challenge of each new day, each new person, when facing joy or pain or uncertainty, enables us to enter more deeply into the grace which helps make the next "yes" easier.

It is not the purpose of this book to discuss methods in detail. There are already many excellent books on that subject, some of which are mentioned in my suggested reading list. But some basic flexible disciplines may be suggested here.

First, there should be time deliberately set apart for prayer each day. If we leave it to our changing moods and emotions, we will certainly not grow in prayer. It is like family life. If a wife cleans, cooks, and shows her loving concern for her husband and children only when she is in the mood for it, we all know what the results are. If we talk with our friends only when we feel like it, we won't be a friend worth having very long. We must decide to make time for praying regularly. We are undertaking real action, real work—it needs real time, as any work does.

Spontaneous prayer at odd moments during the day is very important, too. But prayer means more and arises from a greater depth if there has also been a set time of quiet commitment. Ten minutes regularly every day is far better for growth than two hours one week and none the next. Whether it is morning, noon, or evening is unimportant. It is better to choose a time when not too tired and hungry or too satiated with food. Preferably the quiet time should be in a reasonably quiet place with a shut door if possible. It is well to go regularly to this same place, for the power of association is a great aid.

Bodily posture is unimportant so long as the person is not feeling strained or awkward or self-conscious. Some find the symbolic surrender of kneeling or lying of great help. Others prefer the sitting position as the one in which they can most easily forget the body.

Far more important is bodily relaxation. Tense muscles reinforce the tension of the mind which is a very serious obstacle to the full life of Christ which seeks to flow through us. A slow, steady, gentle breathing helps to achieve relaxation. Likewise, the deliberate loosening of each stiff muscle in turn, especially of the face and the hands, quiets the whole system.

The mental disciplines are more important than the physical, though the two are closely related. The mind should not be encouraged to chatter and jump. The tendency when first learning to pray seriously is to take up several methods of meditation in rapid succession, try to read through three or four books on prayer simultaneously, and clutch eagerly at one meaningful phrase or mental image after another. We must slow down. There is plenty of time. We should move slowly and meditatively through one book at a time. If some sentence seems especially helpful, put the book down, and let the words do their work. The number of devotional books one reads is unimportant. What matters is how profoundly the insight of the author has entered into our understanding.

We should be chary of trying out many different methods and programs. We should choose one that seems well fitted to our own personal circumstances and stick to

71

it firmly but not rigidly. We should always be open to the possibility that Christ might wish to lead us by a new way after a reasonable time of trying the first way.

We should learn an inner silence. A listening, expectant attitude should be cultivated. There will come, after some days or weeks, an inner welling-up of strong certainties, awarenesses, and impressions which we call answers. Perhaps they come from a subconscious wisdom of our own being, brought to light by the silence and relaxed expectancy. Perhaps they are a fresh influx from other sources, whether other people praying for us or thinking of us, or from Christ directly. We are not alone in prayer. We are united in a vast network of sensitive interaction and communication. This is never so true as when we are in the deepest interior silence. We are more aware at those times of the depth of our being touching on the depths of others. For Christians, this communication is swift and profound, for Christ himself, the risen living Christ, holds us together in special union.

Mental images are often helpful in prayer, though they are by no means necessary for everyone. Some choose to think of God in Christ in some pictorial way. Some visualize a scene of healing, or the scene of the resurrection. Some think of a tree and its many branches as a symbol of Christ and those who belong to him. Some imagine the world as resting in the creating hands of God. Some take the image of radiant sunlight or a vast ocean as symbol of the all-encompassing God. When a mental image is found to be helpful, the details should not be unduly elaborated or dwelt upon. The point of any image, whether mental or material, is to trigger a sense of the reality of God for us. We will very likely outgrow our images from time to time as our understanding grows.

It is important to pray for the gift of persons who can help us in this growth in prayer. They should be mature Christians, experienced in prayer. Sometimes these people are called our spiritual guides or directors, but that is a rather solemn name for them. They may well turn out to be the secretary of the minister rather than the minister himself, or a neighbor down the street, or a chemistry professor, or perhaps a member of our own family. These people will come into our lives to help us in our prayer growth when we are ready for them, but we must keep alert to recognize them when they come.

Above all, we must remember that this life of prayer is based on the living Christ. It is not an anxious striving. We need not feel guilty if we lapse—as we will—sometimes for weeks at a time. We are not trying to prove anything, least of all our own worthiness. Christ himself is our goal, and if we surrender to him and keep on surrendering, we have already reached our goal. We are already planted in him, and our prayer life in him is part of a slow maturing process which will take this lifetime and the lifetime beyond to come to the fullness of perfection and fruition. We can relax and rejoice in this. If we have forgotten to pray, we can commend ourselves to Christ and begin again gaily. It is being in him that matters, not how many times we fall down and rise again.

The life of prayer outside the strength of Christ is often a solemn, anxious, heavy striving, where a person feels it is all up to him whether or not he reaches the ineffable Light, and if he fails, he fails. But solemnity is ridiculous in the Christian. He has learned already that he will fail if he stands by himself. That is why he is standing in Christ. That is why Christ came into the world. The Christian has no need to defend himself to his conscience. He can laugh while growing.

II. The Practice
of Christian Prayer

7. The Surprises of Prayer

How often we are surprised in our growing life of prayer! That is one of the surest signs that we have touched reality. I have heard novelists say that sometimes a character in the novel they are writing will seem to come to life in a most disconcerting way and become hard for the author to control. Usually that character is the most living character in the book, because here the author has somehow touched life and not only his own imagination.

Human relationships, if they are healthy and real, also surprise us. We find that our wife or husband or child or friend has a disconcerting "otherness." Their outlook, their action are not merely a reflection of our own. We would "never have guessed it"—what they say and do and become. And if we are mature people we take delight in their otherness and love them anew at a deeper level.

I had a young friend once who had gone through some wretched, tragic experiences. She told me frankly that she had once seriously considered suicide. "What stopped you?" I wanted to know. She thought it over and then said thoughtfully, "Well, I guess it's because life is just so darn surprising. I just had to stay alive to see what's going to happen next!" I wasn't worried any more about her after that. I knew she had a solid hold on reality.

Life with God is the most solid and deep of all reality. So, expect often to be surprised. There are no "textbook cases" in prayer. No one grows according to a set pattern. We are, after all, not mass-produced but hand-crafted, each one of us. God through Christ treasures and develops our personal uniqueness. The more we belong to him, the more we are "ourselves." That, incidentally, is the great difference between the freedom of belonging to God and the bondage of belonging to something else.

The most joyous surprise for me was to discover, as prayer developed, that the material world and other people around me became more interesting and distinct. I had always thought that growing absorption in God would make me more dreamy, absentminded, and indifferent toward the details of daily life. But on the contrary, the material details of the world jumped to life in a most startling way. Colors seemed to become brighter, music became more poignant. Food tasted better. Other people became significant and fascinating. I began to feel that I was for the first time in my life really learning to love my daily life.

And there was a surprising side development to this. As all things became more precious and distinct to me,

78

I found myself becoming more independent of them. For example, though I rejoiced more in a lovely view out of my window, I didn't need that view to keep me happy. Though food tasted better, I didn't eat nearly so much of it as I had before. I began to learn that through Christ we learn to love the world more, appreciate its wonders more, but also become more independent and free of it. It is a love which releases us. Francis of Assisi addressed the powers of nature, fire, water, wind, sun, even death itself, gaily and lovingly as "brother" and "sister." He didn't make the mistake of reverencing them as gods. He loved them and was free of them. Of course we love the world better. Christ himself is the bridegroom of this world, and every bride loves her wedding gifts. But only her bridegroom matters to her overwhelmingly.

Another joyous surprise was the instant strength that came to meet my need when I remembered to ask for it. I have talked to many people who have found the miraculous truth of this. Sometimes things are too strong for us. Greed overwhelms us. Our temper snaps. We go into a panic about something. At this point, if we make the mistake of trying to depend on our own willpower, we will usually fail. If we can remember to call upon the living Christ at that moment, no matter what depth we are in, we will be given the strength we need, instantly.

We mustn't wait for churchlike phrases or appropriate emotions. We mustn't even wait for the thought of Christ's help to seem attractive to us. At the moment of overwhelming emotion or temptation Christ doesn't seem real to us at all. No matter. We can call for help and throw our whole selves trustingly on his reality, whether we feel it to be reality or not.

I have never known it to fail. The response is miraculous. If evidence for the power of prayer is needed, it can be found here. The back of compulsion or fear or temptation is broken, and its hideous strength drains rapidly away. Some of the desire is still there, and we could still surrender with pleasure. But its awesome power over us is gone.

A friend of mine had endangered her health by unwise and excessive eating. She was put on a strict diet and kept to it fairly well by her own willpower. But one day, all of a sudden, she was overwhelmed by a desire to eat something sweet. Her control quite gone, she was already in the kitchen opening the refrigerator door, when she remembered the prayer of "the rope's end." With her hand on the cake box she began praying silently: "God, help me. Please, help me. This cake is more real to me than you are. I can't stop myself. I don't even *want* your help— I'd rather eat this cake. But can you somehow get through to me anyway?" At that moment she felt the terrible compulsion leave her. The thought of the cake was still delicious. She was still hungry. But she no longer felt like a driven slave. It had become again a clear reasonable choice. She shut the refrigerator and went out of the kitchen.

This seems a rather trivial, almost ludicrous example. But nothing, no matter how small, is unimportant if it has become a constant pinprick of self-disgust and tension. The Savior is as concerned with a pebble that stands between us and a full free response to God as he is with a mountain. We need not be ashamed of asking for his power to remove the pebble from our path or the spot from our garment. He will as swiftly and compassionately take over the burden of our disgusting, tempting little faults as he will the burden of some serious sin.

Perhaps this is what Jesus meant by that strange and apparently impractical advice: "Resist not evil." This doesn't mean weak surrender to any person or any temptation that comes our way. Surely he meant that trying to overcome evil merely on the human level with human will and weapons often is a hopeless matter. We are too often swept beyond our depth when we try to fight it on its own ground. Evil is overcome far more swiftly and thoroughly when we admit our weakness and call on the energy of the resurrected Christ to flood the situation with his power.

The only problem is to remember to make this call for help. Christ does not force his protection on us. He works only through our freely surrendered wills. This is one of the major reasons why disciplined surrender in prayer practised daily is so helpful. If we are used to a daily time of letting go of the will and leaning upon the strength of God we will instinctively call for help at times of real emergency.

There are other surprises in prayer. We may find that certain things in our lives are being crowded out. Often they are things which in themselves are innocent and to which we have a moral and legal right, but as we grow spiritually more mature, we may find a growing uneasiness or distaste concerning them. It can be anything: the kind of books we are reading, a club we belong to, something we have been eating or drinking, ways we've been spending leisure time. Generally we will find that changes on our habits brought about by alertness and obedience to the Spirit bring an enrichment of our sharing in the fruits of the Spirit which are "love, joy, peace, patience, kindness, goodness, faithfulness, gentleness, self-control" (Gal. 5:22-23). If the changes within us do not, in the long run, seem to enrich us by these fruits, we had better ask ourselves if the changes truly come from our trust in the living God or if we planned them ourselves.

The most painful surprise in prayer is the fact that at first we seem often to find ourselves growing worse in many ways, more tempted, more sensitive, swifter to anger, fear, and pain.

Actually it is an encouraging sign that our faults seem to grow worse. It means we are growing in reality and seeing ourselves as we truly are. Sometimes certain facts about ourselves are hard to face, but perhaps we could not face them at all if we were not growing by prayer into truth and freedom. The following chapter will give a more detailed discussion on the pain and power of our growing self-awareness through the prayer of reality.

But first a few words on why fear and sensitivity seem also to grow along with prayer at first. This suffering surprises us. As we learn to pray, we learn to love. Perhaps for the first time in our lives our shell of egotism and complacency is broken. We become aware not only of ourselves but of the people around us and their needs and suffering. We may even reach a point where it hurts to read the daily newspaper because of the suffering reported there. Fear for our loved ones may, indeed, increase for awhile, because we have become so much more awakened to the potentialities of pain. To learn to love one person completely, whether friend, parent, husband, wife, child, immeasurably increases our sensitivity to pain. That is why many people are afraid to love at all. Therefore, if through Christ we learn to love many people, then we know we face pain at every corner. The pain of the hurt child we read of in the paper hurts us as much as if that child were next door.

Can we really endure this growing capacity for anguish without being crushed by it? Many idealistic workers have indeed been ground under by their attempt to bear the suffering of the world. But Christians do not undertake this kind of love on their own strength. They stand on the strength of Christ who faced, endured, and overcame the suffering which is the price of love. We are not asked to look helplessly on the pain of the world. Rather, we have the help of the apostle's prayer: "With deep roots and firm foundations, may you be strong to grasp, with all God's people, what is the breadth and length and height and depth of the love of Christ, and to know it, though it is beyond knowledge" (Eph. 3:17-19, NEB).

8. Prayer and Self-awareness

Prayer was never meant to take the place of psychotherapy, but often honest prayer can forestall the need of it. Disciplined prayer, undertaken in the light of the living Christ, not only changes us; it makes us self-aware.

Awareness of one's actual feelings and motives can be an extremely painful process, but it is a necessary process if there is to be health in our religion. Too often, what passes for prayer is used as an escape from the reality of one's actual self. When we escape or hide in this way, by pretending we have certain feelings and motives, we are not building on truth but on dangerous illusion. In such a case, our religion becomes increasingly the greatest obstacle between ourselves and reality. Many psychiatrists have had patients whose false ideas about themselves were reinforced by their religious rationalizations. Such a patient may claim to be upheld by supernatural powers, when in fact, as shown by his defensive, destructive life, he is upheld only by his own desperate neurosis. When, through psychiatry, the patient learns to see himself as he is, he must shed his neurotic religion along with all his other avenues of escape. Too often the patient then concludes that all religion is merely a neurosis and a projection of human needs upon the universe.

However, an understanding of the meaning of prayer in Christ and the disciplined exercise of praying can and does prevent this unhealthy kind of situation.

Very few of us are strong enough to begin our lives in prayer by facing the full truth about ourselves. There are some, to be sure, who have reached the end of their rope, looked with honesty at what they are, and then with a supreme act of faith given themselves over to the mercy of God. The redemptive change that follows such self-abandonment is profound and sometimes startlingly sudden. Indeed, as Jesus said, in such cases "the harlots and the publicans" are able to enter the Kingdom before the wise and good.

But few of us ever reach such a point. We muddle along, living a c-plus life, making resolutions, only halfway keeping them, grabbing a little here, giving a little there, usually too tired and preoccupied to be able to give much thought to the overall picture. A view of the self is apt to be fuzzied over with self-defenses, excuses, and resolutions for the future.

Prayer in Christ helps us to self-honesty. It provides the love and acceptance needed to give us the courage to look at our genuine feelings and our weak points. The Christian dares to do this because he knows he is not meant to walk and grow in his own strength. He is standing in that new stream of unconquerable energy which flows into the world from Christ. Why should he be overly concerned or harassed by revealed weaknesses? He knows that Christ came into the world for the weak and that his grace is made perfect in our weakness. The Christian can stop worrying about what others think of him and what he thinks of himself. "Even if our conscience condemns us, God is greater than our conscience." (I John 3:20, NEB.)

As the Christian becomes increasingly aware of the love surrounding him, he dares to probe deeper and look harder and is given the tools to do so. Many unlovely things may come to light. He may find motives of fear, or envy, or hatred which he never had guessed before. Then he can talk to the strength which comes to meet him: "This is what I am at this moment. This is the feeling I am actually having. You saw it, Lord, before I did. You see it now. It is your love which helps me see it, and I know your love will not only accept it but also change it. At this moment I am unlovely, but I hand myself over to you. Take me off my own hands and deal with me as you will."

Or at the opposite extreme, in the moments of great joy and power and thankfulness, we can also take a long look at our self and pray: "You see my strength and my joy. I thank you for it. I am glad I am given some power and ability to do my work. This is your gift. Take me in

your hands at this moment of my strength and confidence. Hold me by your risen life which is the source of
all strength."

Or in the middle ways, when we are aware of neither
great strength nor weakness but are living as ordinary
human beings, we can, in Christ, see and commit to him
our own ordinariness and our well-meaning mediocrity.
It is humility to see ourselves as commonplace most of
the time. We are never as picturesque as we like to think
we are. It is true humility to see and laugh a little at our
funny self-centered ways, our spurts of generosity, the sudden limitations of the body, the solemn planning of the
future, the childlike desire for amusement, the sulks, the
hopefulness. The person starting the life of prayer is apt to
take these things too seriously. He anxiously examines
every passing mood for signs of sanctity or depravity. But
as he grows in the life of the risen Christ, he will take
these things more lightly and gaily. It will always humili-
ate us a little when our body suddenly lets us down. It will
always be embarrassing when we dig out the self-will
hiding under a noble rationalization. It will always hurt a
little when we know we've made a fool of ourselves, or lost
control of temper or desire. But it is a worse mistake to
take these things too solemnly. Not that they are unimportant. Nothing is unimportant in the life lived in God.
Even small things must be surrendered to him in our love.
But once surrendered they cannot harm us, nor should we
dwell on them too long. We must face them, accept them,
laugh at them, and give ourselves again to Christ who

loves us as we are, yet who has the power and the will to change us.

The greatest of all freedoms is to stop worrying about what God thinks of us or others think of us or what we think of ourselves. It does not matter. At this moment let us put that anxious slavery behind us. We belong to Christ and he will do with us what needs to be done. He will bring forth fruit from us in his own time and his own way.

This is the meaning of the sacrament of confession. We should confess daily, or hourly if possible. Some Christians prefer a special time of uninterrupted self-examination when they can think over the day and really look at what they have done and thought and intended. Others prefer to confess inwardly as they proceed through the day. Either way is a recognition of what is actually going on in the heart. The prayer of self-awareness and confession to God may run along the following lines:

Yes, at that moment I did feel genuine dislike of my child. I couldn't stand one more minute of giving myself to someone else when I wanted so badly to be alone. In fact, I still feel some resentment of how many demands are made on me. You have known this all along, Lord, that I've felt that way. Thank you for helping me see how I was really feeling. I am sorry for any harm it did me or others.

And when that phone call came, I'm so glad that I did feel some genuine love. It seems easier to understand than last week. I'm not exactly proud of my growing love, because, after all, it all comes from you.

I broke that resolution again, Father. I wanted it so badly, I just didn't seem to care what I'd promised. I didn't even stop to pray for strength, because I was afraid you'd *give* me the strength. I wanted to have it more than I wanted strength to resist it. Probably tomorrow I'll want it again. I'll not make any more sweeping promises. Each day I'll give myself to you again for that day only. I'll try to say, "Help me, Lord," before I give in.

But I do get very tired sometimes. Right now it's almost too exhausting to pray. I'm not in the mood, to tell the truth. I know you're here with me, but I can't feel a thing. Yesterday I was feeling so religious, and you seemed so near. Why not now? Well—I belong to you just the same. I know you're working on me even when I can't feel anything, just as when I had that X-ray therapy. I'll just try to relax and *let* you work on me.

I get angry at you sometimes, Father. I almost hated you this morning when I read in the newspaper what happened to that little girl. Why did you let it happen? There are plenty of wicked people who are getting along just fine. If I'd been you I wouldn't have let it happen. But you know all about these feelings of mine, don't you? Perhaps you don't mind angry questions. The Bible is full of them. I guess you know better than anybody all the dreadful things that happen in the world. Maybe this anger came from you first. Maybe I feel it because you want me to feel it. Maybe I wouldn't have felt it so strongly if I hadn't learned something about you, and something about love, and something about prayer. I know very well you were with that little girl and somehow you were suffering along with her. I don't know why such wickedness happens, but I know you are working against it, and that you're holding this world together with your love. I know you're giving everyone of us a new chance every minute. Did you give me this anger I feel? Help me to commit it to you so it can be turned into useful power.

What a wonderful moment that was at noon today, when suddenly everything quieted down and I sat in the lawn chair and watched those birds making a slow circle in the sky. I felt so well, so completed, so thankful. My cup was really running over. Thank you, my Creator, for moments like that. Help me to be grateful for them, help me to take more time each day for them. We are surrounded with such incredible beauty and richness.

But *why* do I react that way when she gets that look on her face and starts tapping her fingers? It makes me feel inside like an angry three-year-old. It's not her fault. It's because she probably reminds me of something, and starts off a whole train of association. You're trying to show me something about myself, Father. What is it? Help me to see what it is, and then help me to do something about it.

Yes, I'd better face it. I *was* relieved when I heard that family wasn't going to move into the house across the street. I was relieved I wasn't going to have to face that problem after all. I can see now that only *part* of me wants your Kingdom to come on earth. I've got a lot of growing to do.

It's been a pretty mixed-up day. But I don't need to be so solemn about it. Help me to laugh a bit at myself. I have every reason to grow more lighthearted, for you've promised to hold me in your hand forever. You've promised to let your life grow more and more in me. Into your hands I give myself again.

9. Prayer and Our Need

Miracles used to embarrass me. At least the New Testament accounts of them did. I would avoid reading them and hurry on to the parts of the Bible that seemed more "spiritual." Miracles were materialistic. They were vulgar. And anyway, I doubted if they had ever happened.

Many educated Christians sidestep the issue of miracles by explaining them as myths. They assume that we of the twentieth century know that such things as miracles do not happen. They concur that the average man two thousand years ago believed in them and took them for granted as part of life. Those legends and exaggerations were suitable to the understanding of people at that time and were the way in which they witnessed to the loving power of God. We, so goes the argument, have other ways of witnessing to that power.

But what about intercessory prayer for our own or other people's material needs? Most ministers do pray, publicly at least, for the needs of others, but probably with the opinion that such a prayer does not have a direct effect on the material environment. Such a prayer is generally explained as being helpful in that it influences the minds of those participating in the prayer. It is the same old stumbling block that we've faced all along, the fact that most of our liberal, well-educated church leaders think of prayer as a subjective thing, a mere state of mind, rather than an actual union with real Power.

Five major obstacles seem to prevent our Christian leaders from taking intercessory and petitionary prayer seriously as a vital part of the Christian life.

The first obstacle may be the underlying feeling that there is something unworthy or at least unimportant about bodily material needs as compared with spiritual needs. Perhaps we feel that there is something selfish or paltry about bringing such needs to God in prayer. However, even the most superficial reading of the Old and New Testaments should prove to us that the biblical approach never regards the body and its needs as unimportant. Jesus treated the plea for bodily health as seriously and generously and with as much dignity as he treated Nicodemus' midnight conversation on the spirit. He fed the multitude with real bread as swiftly and compassionately as he fed them with his counsel and his blessing. He made no distinction whatever between these various needs. Occasionally he hints at an underlying connection between the state of the spirit and the body, and he frequently warned against preoccupation with anxious planning about food and clothing. But need is need, and there is no hierarchy of values in God's swift response. A true mother goes as quickly to her child when he wakes crying from a nightmare as when he is severely injured. God's love ministers to the *whole* person.

A second obstacle may be the thought that whatever is happening might, after all, be the will of God. Perhaps he is sending this sickness or this poverty or this accident as a punishment or a lesson—or at least a trial of our faith and strength. But this is not at all the faith of the New Testament. Jesus never once said to any person asking for healing: "This sickness is God's will for you. You will learn great spiritual lessons from this trial." On the contrary, he taught and showed by his actions that the loving will of God is always on the side of healing. He knew illness, injury, and hunger for what they were—evil. He refers, for example to a deformed woman as one "whom Satan bound for eighteen years" (Luke 13:16). Whatever *we* may believe about the source of evil in the universe, Jesus obviously believed that there were powers of distortion and destruction attacking the very structures of life, and that disease was part of these powers. Where did we ever get the idea that illness might be God's will for us? For centuries it has been taught in Christian churches as sound doctrine, in contrast to the whole spirit of Jesus' words and works. A wild cancerous cell in the physical body is as evil and alien to God's will as the wild malevolent thought in the mind. The starved body of a beggar in India is as agonizing to God as another man's

93

starved personality. The material universe as well as the spiritual must be brought under the redeeming control of Christ.

A third great obstacle in our thinking as we approach petitionary prayer is the fear that we are using God for our own ends. It is quite a popular sermon subject these days to warn people against thinking of God as a giant slot machine or a bigger Santa Claus. We are told that asking God for things is self-centered rather than God-centered. We should be asking only to be drawn nearer his will through a re-creation of our personalities. We are warned against the tendency to magic which uses the laws of God selfishly and impersonally.

But as long as we love him and belong to him, why should not God delight in being used by us? The branch, after all, is using the vine for the ends of its own preservation. A mother delights in being used by her newborn baby. Naturally, it is his will that we should grow to love him as well as to use him. It would be a dreadful waste of creation if we did not mature enough to know the delights of relationship with the Giver as well as the delights of receiving the gifts. The pleasure of knowing him from whom all blessings flow far surpasses all other ecstasy. But this certainly does not mean that the stage of relatively immature demand is unworthy in itself, or that it can be safely bypassed. Far fewer of us are past that stage than we realize. Magic, to be sure is foolish and dangerous. But just as foolish and dangerous is trying to graduate to some spiritual Ph.D. before we've even finished kindergarten. Many seek high mystical experience who do not really believe that God is able to send them even a piece of bread. Many pray for the gift of sacrificial love when it does not occur to them that God might be able to cure their cold. Would not God rather have us use him as spiritual babies than completely ignore one whole aspect of his training and his giving?

From the Christian perspective we never altogether graduate past the "give me, please" stage. We do try to grow in love for the God who gives to us, but along with that maturing love goes the trustful, humble asking for the fulfillment of our needs. The Lord commanded us in his great prayer to ask for our daily bread. Many Christians have never learned to do this. But it means what it says— not spiritual, allegorical, mythical bread but real bread. Food for our hunger. Healing for our diseases. Friends for our loneliness. Work for our livelihood. We need not fear we are merely using him for selfish ends so long as our gratitude and love stretch out to receive the gifts he gives, and so long as our petitions for others are at least as numerous as our petitions for ourselves, and, above all, so long as we put ourselves into his hands daily to be changed by him.

A further major obstacle is the distaste many people feel for this kind of prayer. It seems to them too much like begging and crawling. What kind of God is it who has to be pleaded with before he will do for us what we need done? We all know the kind of person who just loves to be needed by other people and loves to be asked to do

95

things for others so he can feel the satisfactory glow of generosity. Is God really like that? Why should we have to plead with him to make our loved ones well? He knows they are sick. Let him do what he ought to do without our crawling to him!

Unfortunately, many scriptural references do seem to lead to this kind of impression. When we read of God as King, for example, we think of courtiers bowing and presenting petitions or some palace favorite whispering just the right word of influence in the royal ear. Or we read of God as Master, and we think of an overbearing employer granting promotions according to his inscrutable mood. We would have to get "on the right side" of a God like this and make a good impression.

Even the beloved word "Father" raises unfortunate associations and mental images for many. Perhaps we remember severity or indifference from our fathers. Or perhaps we remember our own attitudes—begging for the allowance, wheedling for the car, asking him to get us out of some mess.

Perhaps here the great analogy of the vine and branches will help us. Petitionary prayer is no more begging God to help us than the branch is begging the vine for the life stream. To be sure, the branch is absolutely dependent. Its life and growth come from the vine. But the vine's nature is to give. It "longs" to give. So with God through Christ. It is God's eternal nature to give. He will give us all that we are able and willing to take. Our God is Creator. That means, insofar as we can define him at all,

96

that his essential being is to give, create, flow forth endlessly. He is like the sunlight beating fiercely and radiantly on the closed doors of our little dark selves. He is like the ocean surging over and around the tightly shut shellfish. The more we open up to him, the more his light and his healing will stream into us. As explained before, prayer is learning how to open the tightly shut self and then letting God do what is needed. If personifying images of God cause us difficulties in prayer, it is better to think of him as the endless sea of strength and light.

A final word about this point. Standing within the power of the living Christ, there is no danger that we are crawling or begging when we pray. We are asking *in his name*. There was certainly nothing obsequious or degraded in the way Christ turned himself over to the Father to be the channel of healing to the sick and bread to the hungry. It was done in the most matter-of-fact trustfulness. It was done as if it was the most natural thing in the world that God, the Maker of all things, should so respond to the need of his children. He wished these results of our surrendered wills to be natural. In Christ, we surrender ourselves with dignity.

The last and perhaps most difficult obstacle of all is the deep doubt that this kind of prayer really changes the material world at all. Most educated, liberal Christians are taught from childhood that the age of so-called miracles has passed, and that God expects us to work our own miracles through scientific methods. We are taught that he has made the laws of nature and will not break them for our personal benefit. We all know people who have prayed earnestly for healing and yet have died. We know that through recorded history the innocent have suffered in famine, disease, and disasters. And we know these horrors happened in spite of prayers. So, sadly, most modern Christians have concluded that it may be effective to pray for one's emotional outlook, or to pray for someone else's state of mind if he happens to be listening; but to change the state of the body or the material world we had better depend only on the physician, the police, the government, and on our own good sense and hard work. God has made his laws, and he works through them.

But as we discussed earlier, are we so sure we know what *are* God's deepest laws? What would seem like the breaking of a natural law to a primitive man would be considered by a doctor a deeper understanding and better use of the law. There are times, and many of them, in our human situation when the inexplicable breaks through in a way which cannot seem to be explained by our observation of natural law. We have been taught, even by our Christian churches, that this doesn't happen; that it is fraud, self-deception, or coincidence, or "just one of those things." But these things do happen. They happen frequently and astonishingly when surrender and discipline in Christ-centered prayer is undertaken by an individual or a group.

Any person, no longer content merely to preach against the whole concept of miracle, who will simply and perhaps secretly set out to experiment in this realm of faith will

98

find many surprises. It should not be approached defiantly or hysterically. At the beginning one had better choose an ordinary time when there is no great sorrow, pain, or fear, but just the daily task of life at hand. Let him relax body and mind. Let him remember that the great prayer of Christ to the Father is everlasting and he, the member of Christ, is merely opening his being to this mighty force. Let him commit certain problems trustfully to this surging power of God. It may be a prayer for his aunt's headache, and he can visualize her surrounded by the healing strength of Christ. Let him silently commit an angry or frightened person wholly to the care of God, or give over to God the destructive attitudes poisoning some group meeting. Let him pray about some item in the newspaper which catches his attention and sympathy. Let him turn over to God some slight illness in his own body or some nagging worry in his mind.

Naturally we continue to use our hands, our intelligence, our doctor's care if indicated, our common sense always. But at the same time, inwardly, we should visualize the problem, the pain, the illness, the quarrel, whatever the need, as something resting in the hands of Christ, committed by our surrender to his concern and power. We can pray simply and directly concerning this need every day, but we should not concentrate on the need or problem itself. Rather, we should concentrate on the power of God through Christ which is sufficient for this need. Above all, we must remember that illness and accident are never the will of God for men. Christ healed everyone who asked him.

Anyone who experiments honestly with an open mind, genuinely desiring to learn something new, believing in the kind of God that Christ showed us, will soon discover beyond any possibility of doubt that the age of miracles is not over. Every Christian, thus praying, could write his own book of Acts. There are many such books full of interesting evidence. Some of them are listed in the bibliography. But far more convincing is for each Christian to find his own evidences.

Sometimes it seems that our prayer has not been granted—at least in the way that we expected. We do not know why. There may be factors in the situation we don't know about. There may be unconscious obstacles in ourselves or other people. God will not force his gifts upon us, and often we are pushing away with one hand what we are reaching for with the other. We must know ourselves and our true wishes better than we generally do. Above all, we must know that our human community is a closely knit web of relationships. The innocent do suffer with the guilty. The seeds cast by one are reaped by others as well. As long as we are in this world, bound to our brothers, this cannot be altogether avoided. We will continue to bear one another's burdens and guilt. God's answer must come to us often through the distorted medium of the badly fractured situation and often through unconsciously resisting persons.

But there will always be an answer. There will be some

100

kind of improvement and healing in any problem committed to God by a surrendered group or individual. The healing may not always be complete, but there will be some changes for the better after a while.

For example, we knew a young woman dying of incurable cancer. A committed prayer group prayed earnestly and constantly for her. She herself attended the prayer group when possible. She did not live, but after she learned to surrender herself in trustful prayer the pain left her, and she died in peace without needing drugs of any kind. She knew that a fuller life was opening before her, and she went to it with joy and confidence. This was a complete healing of the spirit and a partial help to the body.

There are other examples of partial healing in a situation of broken relationships. A fine, well-educated young man with an excellent professional life ahead of him underwent the tragedy of an unhappy and broken marriage. In his misery he quarreled with his friends, began using alcohol as an escape, lost his job, and lost any rights to his children. His life seemed wrecked. But the prayer group of his church refused to give up hope, and earnestly in their thoughts held him in the merciful light of God. They knew that with God nothing is hopeless. As the months went on, the young man pulled himself together emotionally and physically. He is working again. He is again, full of hope and confidence in life. His marriage is still broken and many relationships are lost or badly scarred. Perhaps they will never be healed in this life.

101

But *he* is healed. God made a new creation in the midst of total ruin.

We can always pray with expectancy. God does not demand a mountain of faith—merely a mustard-seed amount of trust. At times we can't help being afraid or doubtful. God understands this, and we need only confess our natural fear and commit that to him too. Answers will come. Sometimes they will be all we asked for. Sometimes only in part. Sometimes they will be completely unexpected answers. But answers there will be. He is still the vine. We are still the branches.

10. Prayer
and the Cross

Long ago I read the autobiography of Chakkarai, a Hindu convert to Christianity, *Jesus the Avatar*. When asked what one thing in Christianity finally tipped the scales for him, Chakkarai answered it was the cross. There were miracles, wise words, noble example, and incarnations to be found all through Hinduism, but nothing at all corresponding to the cross and its meaning. That he had found only with Jesus, and it changed everything.

Perhaps it was this cross which kept our faith from becoming just another occult mystery religion, in which the devotee learns to worship the power and beauty of his God and to get the most out of him but is not bound to him by the ties of love and suffering. Our God did not merely share his gifts with us; he faced the ultimate blackness of evil and despair for us and then broke its hideous strength. There in Gethsemane, Jesus was looking at something much worse than a painful physical death.

He who could read the hearts and thoughts of men, who could see life with the lid off, so to speak, could certainly see evil and cruelty for what it was. We see it with the merciful blinders of our five senses, in the context of limited time and space. But he saw it in its naked being; the rotting leprous heart of all that hates and rebels against its Maker. We can't even imagine what such a sight would be like, anymore than we can imagine the true face of God. But even as Jesus saw God, he could see anti-God. And the sight was enough to make him weep with fear.

But he bore that ultimate horror for us as he had borne everything else—fatigue, temptation, pain, misunderstanding. And since then, the horror has never had the ultimate word over those who have taken their refuge in him who loved us.

There is no tie greater than that which binds us to one who has suffered for us. I wrote down Chakkarai's words:

Such love as this was, in the Christian consciousness of Jesus, not an external thing bestowed on him, but it was the very lifeblood of his being. In it bhaktas hear the very beats of his mighty heart, and through them the very beats of God's heart itself. . . . It does not dawn on the individual with lightning flash but gently, yet with the power of God. It then grips and then does not let go. . . . Once a man has known him truly to some extent, he can never forsake him. He becomes the very life of his life, and it is not the disciple that lives but Christ that lives in him.

The same recognition of the suffering love of Christ was equally beautifully expressed by another Hindu, the great Sri Ramakrishna. He never became a Christian, but he had had a vision of Jesus once, and through him felt he had come to a deeper understanding of God. He wrote, after envisioning the Christ: "Behold the Christ, who shed his heart's blood for the redemption of the world; who suffered a sea of anguish for love of men. It is he, the Master Yogi, who is in eternal union with God. It is Jesus, love incarnate." [1]

I have always been touched by that phrase "Master Yogi" used in reference to Jesus, just as naturally as one of the Jewish or Moslem faith would refer to a "great Prophet." Master Yogi he was indeed. He knew all there was to know about the experience of mystical union, miracles, and all the charismatic gifts. But as Ramakrishna recognized, here was a yogi who went beyond such things though he was master of them all. He "suffered a sea of anguish for love of men."

This is why we love him. And this is why the Christian can never get so carried away with the delights of miracles, healing powers, answered prayer, that he forgets the cross which was the central meaning for Jesus and is the central meaning for us if we are truly in him and of him.

As pointed out before, there is certainly nothing wrong or selfish in asking God for daily bread in a very literal

[1] *The Gospel of Sri Ramakrishna*, tr. and ed. Swami Nikhilananda (New York: Ramakrishna-Vivekananda Center, 1958), p. 59.

sense. Our God is Father, and it is his eternal nature to meet our needs as Father to child. But the Christian makes these petitions in the context of belonging to Christ. All things are ours, Scriptures tell us, but we are Christ's. That means we share in the cross.

What is this cross? How does it concern us? First we must know what it is not. It is not illness. God never laid an illness on any human being and told him to bear it as a cross. Jesus looked on illness as the work of Satan and healed everyone he possibly could. It is a misfortune if we are ill. If healing is delayed we can certainly, with God's help, turn it to a blessing. But it is not the same as the cross.

It is not accident. Accident, like illness, is not an "act of God," whatever legal terms may say. It is a tragic reaping of thoughtlessness. Sometimes it is part of the price we pay for living in a universe of limitation, whose laws we do not yet fully understand. Many prayer adepts have come to think that spiritual growth means a lessening of the likelihood of accident since our sensitive awareness of situations increases.

The cross is nothing thrust upon us against our will, which we are forced to undertake for survival or under legal or social pressure. We all have occasional illnesses. We all have occasional accidents. We all have things we have to do, like it or not. But these are not the Christian's cross.

The cross is the free choice, deliberately taken in Christ, to be the concerned sharer and bearer of another's burden and being. It is a chosen self-giving. It is a chosen responsibility. It may not always be painful. It may sometimes give great joy. But it is on us, and when we have taken it, it is not something we can lay down when we are not in the mood. We have chosen, as those belonging to Christ, to let him change us, work through us, empower us to love and serve our brothers and bear their burdens.

We believe that to choose this is to set us fathoms deeper into the heart and the meaning of God than the choice of using our very real powers for any other end could do. To belong to a church, to learn of prayer does not necessarily commit us to this decision. This does not condemn those who put their creative gifts, their powers of organization, their brilliant intellects, their understanding of human nature at the service of some other end than bearing the cross of the world's suffering in compassion. No, it is not to condemn these, for they have often accomplished much in their own way in the advancement of art, knowledge, inventiveness, government. But we claim, nevertheless, that any person, no matter how great and gifted, who has not chosen to share the cross of love for others has not yet reached the heart of God's meaning.

The would-be Christian must ask himself deliberately whether he actully is willing to be Christ's. He must ask himself what this belonging means. "Let us sit at your right hand and your left," said James and John to Jesus, knowing well what tremendous mastery over life this man had. Naturally they wanted to be in on the secrets and the power. The adherents of the mystery religions, so widespread in the Empire at that time, felt this way. "Open the mystery to us. Let us be knowers—Gnostics— of the depths, so we may be masters over ourselves, others, and all of life." And Jesus answered then as he does now: "Do you know what you are asking? You want to enter *my* secrets, and be *my* men? Then you must be able to drink the cup I drink and be baptized with the same baptism. To enter into my secrets is, indeed, to enter into great power but also into great pain. That is the way I give myself to the world."

If we belong to someone else, this ultimate way may not be demanded of us. We can seek the gifts and secrets and be content in personal unfolding. But if we belong to Jesus and possess the secrets and the powers in his name, then every day, in one way or another, we must lift the burden for others and share as deeply in their pain and their being as they permit us. To wish and be empowered to do this, is to know God as man has never before known him.

Sometimes this daily cross is a simple thing, such as listening carefully and compassionately to someone's problem. As Christ's man, we now answer the phone, open the door, open a letter or the newspaper, or turn to greet a friend on the street in a different spirit than before. It may be Christ, here summoning us to meet a need. Or it may be a gravely demanding challenge; working against some social injustice or suffering even at the cost of unpopularity or fatigue or finanical loss. Or the cross in our case may imply the free, deliberate changing of our personal attitude toward some difficult, distasteful task or duty. For example, if it seems best to take some sick or aged relative into our home, we can either set our teeth and endure it grimly, or we can embrace the situation, giving with love the best we have. Or if our daily work brings us into contact with some disagreeable person, we have the free choice of either "putting up with it" as one of the necessary evils of life, or changing our attitude toward that person by praying for him and looking for the best in him.

In any case, the cross implies a free situation. We always have the choice of escaping it literally or emotionally, or of accepting what is asked in the love and strength of Jesus. After a while it becomes almost instinctive with us, this new attitude toward events, in which we ask, "Am I needed here? What can I learn from this? What is God trying to tell me?" It becomes truly part of our own nature to try to lower walls that divide us from other people, and to thrust our hands over those walls saying, in effect, "I am here, hold onto me."

This does not mean that the Christian himself is by nature necessarily loving, warmhearted. Many Christians have had to learn through Christ to be loving. It did not come easily or naturally at all. And even the more fortunate types who are naturally affectionate and responsive will sometimes not wish to be bothered by other people. But we are not asked to take the attitude of the loving cross by our own strength of love. There will be times when we are almost galled and fatigued beyond endurance by meeting the needs of others. Then only the swift gift of our wills to Jesus can flood us again with strength and freedom. When it seems impossible for us to love the person before us, we must learn to let go inwardly and ask *Christ* to do the loving through us. Remember always, he is not asking us to be perfect lovers. He is already the perfect lover. He is asking us to surrender to him, so he can be the lover of that unattractive person through us. The response to this kind of prayer is swift, miraculous, and quite unmistakable in the effect it has in the situation and in our own feelings.

Prayer in Christ is thus deeply linked with the cross. Not only are we enabled to bear any cross, we are also empowered to bear more of the cross. Intercessory prayer, for example, is one of the most profound ways of carrying another's burden. In some situations, praying for another is the only thing we can do, and many times it is the best thing to do.

We must remember when praying for another that prayer is not merely an emotional state of mind but an actual force, a power which is being let loose into the world through us. It is not a power we are creating. As Christians, we believe that the great intercessory prayer for healing and renewing is eternally flowing from Christ the Son to the Source of all being—the Father, and that the loving response forever flows through Christ to the created world. Christians by praying link themselves to that power which is Christ's prayer. We are opening ourselves to its radiance and its force. We are becoming like lightning conductors to channelize this loving power to the person for whom we pray.

When he omits prayer, the Christian only half helps his brother, in spite of all the talking and working he may do. The greatest thing he can do for another in his love and concern is to discipline himself to commit that person to the light of Christ. We should not concentrate on problems or illness, but rather place the *whole* person, the *whole* situation trustfully in God's hands as one "to whom all things are possible." We are to take on this burden regularly, no matter how slow the answer seems to be in coming, and keep an expectant attitude. It is also extremely important to give joyous thanks regularly for any growing improvement. Remember, we are not thanking God for having changed his mind because we begged him to. We are thanking him because he is the God of love and healing who is responsible for any good thing we allow to break through to us. We are thanking him because it is his will that we be whole, even though his full will is so often unfulfilled in our human situation. Every time we give ourselves to him his will breaks through and is made manifest.

Those for whom we pray need not be only those well known to us. Often God will put on us the responsibility for someone quite unknown. It may be some stranger we see in the bus whose face is unhappy. It may be the clerk in the store whose tired voice reaches us over the phone. It may be the picture of someone in the paper or an article about some stranger. But for some reason, we know God has laid this person on our heart. We may be called to pray for him just that once, or we may feel impelled to do so for years.

To join in Christ's great prayer for the healing of the world is often a joy but is always a cross. Every Christian is summoned to this kind of prayer, no matter what his kind of personality or what his special strengths. No matter who or what we are, Christ can use us for the suffering world if we only give ourselves to him.

11. The Prayer of Feasting

There is one kind of prayer which is rather neglected by Christian writing and even a bit suspect in some circles. It has many names, and its extremes have been found in many religions. It is called the prayer of worship or the prayer of passion or, as I prefer, the prayer of feasting. It is the prayer which arises when the worshiper is overwhelmed by the ecstasy and beauty of God. It is an intoxicating experience of God's mystery. Many are led to God first by this path, sometimes through the beauty of nature or some form of art. It is not uniquely Christian, because it was experienced long before Christianity in many different ways. But it is not anti-Christian either.

I first got an inkling of this kind of prayer when as a child I heard the magnificent old hymn, written so many centuries ago, "Jerusalem the Golden":

> They stand, those halls of Zion,
> All jubilant with song,

> And bright with many an angel,
> And all the martyr throng;
> The Prince is ever in them;
> The daylight is serene;
> The pastures of the blessed
> Are decked in glorious sheen.
>
> There is the throne of David;
> And there, from care released,
> The shout of them that triumph,
> The song of them that feast.

I remember thinking as I sang about the singing and the shouting that this was a very different kind of Heaven than that of resigned harp playing and hushed "Sabbath" voices that I had somehow envisioned. This struck a genuine note of ecstasy that surprised me.

I ran across the same note of exultation some years later when, browsing through the Old Testament, I saw these words in Zephaniah:

> Sing aloud, O daughter of Zion;
> Shout, O Israel!
> Rejoice and exult with all your heart, . . .
>   The Lord, your God, is in your midst,
> A warrior who gives victory;
>   He will rejoice over you with gladness,
> He will renew you in his love;
>   He will exult over you with loud singing
> As on a day of festival. (Zeph. 3:14, 17, 18.)

It is a good thing for a child to realize that the love of God involves singing, shouting, dancing, feasting, utter rapture. Why is it so often neglected in our preaching and teaching?

Gerald Heard explains it this way:

Because with our Hebrew background and medieval middle distance, because to the Jew, God was Justice and the Law, and to the Christian He was Sacrifice, we have neglected His third attribute, Beauty. So it may well be that in our reaction to beauty it is that we shall best come to understand the nature of worship and praise. . . . When we see supreme beauty, either in nature or in art, we do not—we cannot—ask, of what use is it? What could it do for me? or, How much does it demand of me? . . . We are arrested, rapt, altered. In our unguarded self-forgetfulness we "give ourselves away." [1]

Has this kind of joy a place, indeed, in the Christian context of suffering love ? We have seen hints of it in the Old Testament—the passage from Zephaniah, many of the Psalms, the symbols of radiant bride and bridegroom in the Song of Solomon, David, the King, dancing in ecstasy before the Ark of the Lord. But in the New Testament, where the cross is the center?

We do, indeed, seem a bit doubtful of it. Our Call to Worship and opening hymn are traditionally the time of exultant praise and delight in God, but we rarely sound convinced. "The chief purpose of man is to glorify God

[1] *A Preface to Prayer*, p. 154.

and enjoy Him forever," goes the great Confession. Our meaning is to enjoy *him*, not merely his works or the fruits of his Spirit. I sometimes think the restless discontent our young people feel concerning the church and the great curiosity about the aesthetic and mystical experiences under the psychedelic drugs have some connection with our neglect of the worship experience in our Christian churches. Yet it is there at the heart of the New Testament, implicit, undeniable.

We may be reasonably sure that the man Jesus, whose love and power over life were stronger than storms, disease, death, and the very heart of evil itself, was a man who knew everything about the burning, creative, rejoicing heart of God as well as the suffering heart of God. We have such tantalizing hints as that account of the blazing whiteness of his face on the Mount of Transfiguration, which gives some indication of the wedding feast perpetually in his heart with his Creator.

G. K. Chesterton develops this into a fascinating approach:

> Joy which was the small publicity of the pagan is the gigantic secret of the Christian. . . . The tremendous figure which fills the Gospels towers in this respect. . . . He never concealed his tears. . . . He never restrained his anger. . . . Yet he restrained something. I say it with reverence; there was in that shattering personality a thread that must be called shyness. There was something that he hid from all men when he went up a mountain to pray. There was something he covered constantly by abrupt silence or impetuous isolation. There was one thing that was too great for God to show us

116

when he walked upon our earth; and I have sometimes fancied that it was his mirth.[2]

The Christian may, through Christ, find God not only as Father and Shepherd, but also as lover and bridegroom. He may learn to think of union with that God not only as coming home to the compassionate, forgiving Father, but as the ecstatic dance of eternal youth, with the eternal God, the Ancient of Days himself as the heart and leader of all youth and springtime.

Fra Angelico grasped this in the brilliant colors of his dancing souls in Paradise. Bach translated ecstasy into music in his Sanctus in the B Minor Mass. William Blake witnessed to this in his great drawing of God and the soul of man embracing in a storm of flames at the end of his poem *Jerusalem*.

Man was made for ecstasy as well as for suffering and quiet reasonable affection. The God who has created the beauty of art, music, great mountains and sunsets, sexual union, and the whole thrust of evolving nature certainly never intended us to live solely in cautious rationality. We only half know him if our hearts have never danced in his beauty.

How much we miss the point when we think of worship as something we give to God because he needs it. "How can one want to spend eternity being thanked and praised?" I heard someone remark in all sincerity the other

[2] G. K. Chesterton, *Orthodoxy* (London: John Lane Company, 1908), pp. 298-99.

117

day. "What sort of God is it who wants to be praised and flattered all the time!" That is similar to saying: "How egocentric of the air to insist that we breathe it all the time!" The deepest breath of life comes to the soul and body of man when he grows in praise and thankfulness. God does not need it. We need it.

The ability to adore, to find rapture in the awareness of him, is the gift of God to the whole being of man in his growing responsiveness. Without it we are only half awake, barely conscious, living only in the outermost levels of our nature. There is much talk these days about "man come of age" without the need of religious reference. What a pathetic misunderstanding of the being of man. No matter how technically skilled we may be, no matter how adjusted to our needs and our environment, no matter how adept we have become at living in kindly peace with other people, we have not yet learned the depths of what we are until we have feasted and danced in the joy of the Lord.

In a way, of course, we are thanking and adoring God when we use his gifts heartily and healthfully. The rejoicing over a good meal, a happy marriage, a return to health are, even without conscious thankfulness, joining the feast of joy at a primitive level. But it compares to the joy of awareness as the healthy contentment of a well-fed baby compares to the ecstasy of a great painter. The baby *is* happy. But its happiness is of a different order from that of the painter.

It is foolish and unrealistic to insist that only religious

118

people are happy and that all others are subconsciously miserable. This is our modern, liberal way of calling men to conversion rather than by the old orthodox way of threatening them with hellfire. Basically, however, the two methods are not so different. They both insist that without awareness of God, man is hopelessly miserable. But I think the facts are against us. I have known many happy pagans. We drive home from church and see them puttering around in their gardens, glancing up at us with sunny smiles. They are very happy indeed with their gardens, their good health, their children. We put ourselves laughably in the wrong when we urge them to face their inner misery and despair and come to God for happiness.

"But I'm *not* miserable and despairing," our gardening neighbor may reply quite reasonably. "I'm perfectly happy already. I don't need your God to find peace of mind." And he may be quite right, according to his definition of happiness.

How much better to admit his level of happiness. How much wiser to admit he has found a well-adjusted life. But then we can take the next step and tell him of (or better yet, *show* him) another kind of happiness on a different level, a different dimension. It does not negate his former joy. It fulfills it. It is the kind of joy which will bring him to a wakefulness and awareness which he has never experienced before.

It is interesting to observe in the Scriptures of all the great religions of the world, how repeatedly the motif of *waking up* is stressed as the soul matures. We are left with the impression that most of us in this life are in a semiconscious, dreaming state compared with the full wakefulness of the God-possessed man or woman. And without exception they describe their times of full wakefulness, full awareness as utter ecstasy and unspeakable rejoicing. Then they turn with compassion to the rest of us, wrapped in our sleep and our dreams. Some of us are having nightmares. Some of us are having genuinely happy dreams. But even at their best they are but dreams compared to the full life which could be ours if we but let ourselves be wakened.

The Christian who has never known the prayer of feasting, the genuine thankfulness and joy, is but half awake, no matter what his creed. The ability to adore is a gift, yes. But it is a gift which God offers every minute of the day. We have but to learn to receive it.

As with all prayer in the name of the living Christ, it is based first of all on trustful faith. We must believe Christ knew what he was talking about when he said: "These things I have spoken to you, that my joy may be in you, and that your joy may be full" (John 15:11). We must commit ourselves to the trust that he experienced joy, and that he is able, as the risen Christ, to share his joy with us. Our adoration can be based on this trust even when we are not at the moment in a joyful mood at all. We ask him to take us into his field of radiant energy and enable us to look with joy to the Mystery he calls Father.

Then in relaxed silence we let him do for us what we have asked him to do.

As we wait expectantly in the light of Christ, we begin to see the Father as he saw him. We begin to see that the Mystery which holds us is likewise aware of us. It loves us. It will never let us go. It seeks our response and the awareness of our glance. We begin to know that "the more your heart loves, the more it desires, and the more it desires the more it finds. The will of God presents itself at each instant like an immense ocean which the desire of your heart cannot empty, although it will receive of that ocean the measure to which it can expand itself by faith, confidence, and love." [3]

Then genuine joy and thankfulness begin to creep into our hearts. The whole context of prayer changes when we allow ourselves time for the faith of Christ to work on us and awaken us. Perhaps we had entered the time of prayer anxious, tense, full of requests and intercessions. But as we become aware of the surrounding love which offers us far more than we are capable of receiving, our tensions and haste and pressure relax. The growing power of adoration which begins to lift us is the power which enables us later to enter into intercession without anxiety and strain.

This is extremely important for a prayer group as well as for an individual, as I learned recently. In our church prayer group some of us had noticed that the power and joy which filled our prayer eight months ago when our

[3] Jean Pierre de Caussade, *Self-abandonment to Divine Providence* (Springfield, Ill.: Templegate Publishers, 1959), p. 23.

group was born had seemed to diminish. The time together was both more tense and more monotonous. What had happened? One of our members thoughtfully said: "We are centering more and more around our requests and petitions. Our prayer list is so long. We seem to leave so little time for thankfulness and adoration."

She had put her finger right on the trouble. We were so filled with the thought of God using us as channels and instruments of his healing will, that we had not offered him time to open those channels and sharpen those instruments by the power and the beauty of his presence. Yes, even we who pray are often guilty of "leaving Christ and entering his service instead." We are now trying to learn to *ask* only in the context of *adoring*. He can't do much through us until we are aware of his love and respond to that love.

Then there are the many moments through the day, when we don't have time to sit in silence, when we can express the dancing prayer of joy through swift thankfulness for the gifts of the Father. As we take them and heartily use them, the bread, the water, the flower, the letter that came, the faces and voices we love, we can learn to turn the loving glance for a moment to the Father, even when there is no time for words. What counts is the surge of awareness that every moment is a precious gift from his hands.

It is a discipline—this learning the prayer of feasting. We have to learn deliberately how to pray in joy and grow through adoration, just as we have to learn deliberately how to recognize and serve our neighbor. Few of us are born with the ability to rejoice in the beauty of the Lord, just as few of us are born with the willingness to take up the cross of sacrifice. But both are implied in being Christ's man, "who for the joy that was set before him endured the cross" (Heb. 12:2).

But it is a discipline undertaken in his risen life. He, the master of joy as well as "the man of sorrows," will teach us the steps of the dance and bring us to the feasting.

There is a wonderful prayer contained in the Hebrew Morning Service:

Though our mouths were full of song as the sea, and our tongues of exultation as the multitude of its waves, and our lips of praise as the wide-extended firmament; though our eyes shone with light like the sun and the moon, and our hands were spread forth like the eagles of heaven, and our feet were swift as hinds, we should still be unable to thank thee and to bless thy name, O Lord our God and God of our fathers, for one thousandth or one ten thousandth part of the bounties which thou hast bestowed upon our fathers and upon us.

It is quite true. Though we reached the peak of adoration which our whole awakened hearts could offer, we still could not express it all. But Christ, the master of joy, not only brings us to the beginnings of thankfulness, he takes it up where we must leave off and carries our feeble prayers in strength to the central fire of God.

12. Prayer and Eternal Life

Survival beyond the grave is one thing. Eternal life is quite another. Ordinary survival after death is not an exclusively Christian concept. Most religions have taught it in one form or another; actually it is not in itself a religious doctrine at all. If some day it could be proved scientifically that our personalities survive death in some form, it would not necessarily prove anything about God or immortality. As the psychical researcher G. N. M. Tyrrell says:

It is unconsciously assumed that if we pass away from this present world we must pass at once into a *religious* sphere. . . . But suppose that at death we do not leave the "natural realm" at all; or suppose, rather, that no hard and fast line separates the "natural" from the "supernatural." . . . After all, the idea that dying does not launch us into a religious sphere is quite simple when once we have grasped the idea that "nature" need not come to an end where it ceases to be visible.[1]

[1] *The Personality of Man* (Baltimore: Penguin Books, 1947), p. 278.

Therefore it would be quite possible for dreary, self-centered, narrow-minded Mrs. Jones to enter the next life with exactly the same dreary narrowness she carried around with her in this life. Physical death in itself would not change her unless she wished to be changed. We can resist change in ourselves forever if we wish. I remember the excitement and glamour of my first job, as a student minister in Wyoming. I was far away from home, with a completely different kind of work to do and a completely different landscape surrounding me. I was sure life also would be completely changed from that moment on. I would be a different person. But to my surprise and consternation, after the excitement of the first week or two had died down, I found I was the same old self with exactly the same exasperating faults. Everything around me was changed—but only I could change myself.

We make the same disconcerting discovery when we marry, when our children are born, when we move to a new town. The old self comes along. The unfortunate people who never really grow up never understand or accept that. Because they are fed up with themselves, they keep childishly changing jobs, or wives, or houses, hoping that the miracle will happen and they will become what they want to become.

What they are really looking for is the New Creation, which usually comes as a quiet decision in the midst of accustomed, ordinary life. At that point we enter eternal life, whether in this world or the next. It has nothing to do with the moment of physical death. Physical death is only one among many incidents in the long path of development.

Perhaps it can be compared to the transplanting of a shrub. We will be carried to a different soil in a different garden, but this physical change will not effect the flow of life from the stem to the branches. That flow of life is already established. The swift change of soil and surroundings is but an external unimportant incident.

Eternal life is actually our decision to let the life of God flow into and through us. When we choose this, we are reborn that very moment. In this life we are still enclosed and permeated by time, space, and the limitations of our physical body, but we are no longer possessed by this world. When we die, we will enter into other faculties in a different kind of body, perhaps in a different kind of matter. But we won't be any closer to the love of God than we are at this moment. Already in this life, if we belong to Christ we belong to the eternal Father as much as we will ever belong. He will do greater works through us as we progress. We will behold vaster, yet unimaginable beauty. But already in this embryonic state we are in him and of him, and his love for us will never be deeper than it is now.

For this reason, communion with those in Christ who have physically died becomes the obvious, unremarkable thing it was meant to be. This is not to be interpreted as a recommendation of spiritualism, interesting though that movement is and indicative of the neglected hungers in our Protestant churches. The communion of saints is part of the creed and was held to be literal fact in the early Christian church. If a man or woman was in Christ, what difference did it make if he was in this mortal body or in another unseen body? He was still close. He could be prayed with and for, and still loved. Why are we so frightened and repelled at that thought? I once attended a church discussion group during a Lenten series on the statements in the creed. The subject for this particular evening was death and eternal life. A distinguished professor of theology and the minister of the church led the discussion. At one point in the evening, as the talk was becoming increasingly vague, general, and theoretical, a sensible looking woman arose and said plainly that she knew the communion of saints was a fact, because she had often been helped in many ways by her sister who had died years earlier. She went on to give several instances and evidences of this help and presence. Though the professor and minister kept interested, courteous smiles on their faces, I could almost see them inwardly shuddering with distaste. "What I am sure you are trying to say," the professor said cautiously when she had finished, "is that the living God has helped you and been close to you, and that *represents* your sister's love to you. After all, your sister is in him now. She is committed to his hands, and whatever she wishes to do for you is done through God now."

It was perfectly obvious from what he said that the dead were no longer real to him. They had somehow ceased to be full persons who love and act and make choices. We could no longer have dealings with persons who had died. He implied that if we tried to relate to them still as persons, we were being rather morbid and unchristian. After all, now they are committed to God.

But were they not, in this life, also committed to God? Did that make them less real to us? Did that cut off real communion and sharing and love with us? Do we think because the body has died that they have gone instantly into such a state of perfection that they no longer need our prayers, or into such a state of indifference or pre-occupation that they no longer care for us and pray for us? What a loss it is and what insult to the constant love and help that streams between us to consider them broken off from us!

We Protestants should rethink our whole position on this neglected doctrine of the communion of saints. I am not suggesting séances or ouija boards. But I am suggesting that we continue daily to pray for those we love who are risen in Christ; that we think often and lovingly of them, not as memories but as living realities; that we mentally and prayerfully share our problems with them and ask for their help, knowing they still care. They, too, have much growing to do, and we can help them more than we realize. Their strength can join ours to make a greater strength, and their prayer can join ours to make a stronger prayer. We can encourage one another to make forever a deeper surrender to Christ.

Friends of ours had a four-year-old daughter who died of

a brain tumor. Observing through the months the progress of this illness, I was astounded at the peacefulness of the young mother. She grew very thin and pale as time went on, but she faced the illness and death of her child with unflinching calm. She talked about her child after the death freely and frequently. There was nothing strained or morbid in these references. She referred to this child no oftener than she referred to her two other children, and it was obvious that Mary who had died was still her child. She was as matter-of-fact about it as if the child had gone away on a trip to visit relatives. "You sometimes feel Mary with you?" I asked once as we sat in the kitchen. "Yes, of course," she said. "And I know Mary is going to help us all more and more as time goes on." Mary was still part of her life. She knew God had not separated them. There was a place in his Kingdom for her motherhood and Mary's childhood.

The only fact that really matters is that we belong to him. His life bursts within us as the seed bursts in the ground and thrusts itself into the light. His radiant energy carries us with its force. We lift our little prayers with boldness. We are not overly concerned about our weakness, because our "yes" is all that matters. Carried by those mighty hands, fed by that bread, we are all, whether in the body or out of the body, at the very heart of Meaning.

13. How Can We Help the Church?

The first step in helping the church through prayer is to realize what is the quickest way to *harm* the church. And that is to try "to go faster than grace," as Brother Lawrence has warned in his letters on the "Practice of the Presence of God."

All spiritually mature leaders of prayer warn us against this fault. It is such a temptation for the person who has just begun serious prayer to believe he has a special calling and gift to change his church, to change his minister, to change everyone around him, before he himself is genuinely changed. He tries to organize prayer groups; he listens impatiently to the thoughts of those who do not yet see his point of view; he makes great claims which have yet to bear fruit in his own life.

The greatest mistake we can make is, after discovering the power of prayer in our own lives, to try to bring it into other lives through our own strength and efforts.

We can test this inclination in ourselves by noticing our own mounting tension and emotional involvement as we try to persuade others to a life of prayer. If we have truly learned to depend upon the power of the risen Christ, there will not be this urgency and inner pressure. There will be a relaxation, a poise, a lightness of touch. There will even be an ability to laugh. We will be able to listen quietly to the other person, even if we do not agree with him. We will be willing to be interrupted and challenged. We can afford to "let go" inwardly, even in the midst of our deep concern, and leave the issue to Christ. It is he, not ourselves, who brings forth the fruit of another's conversion.

It does not all depend on us! What an utter freedom, relief, and release to realize that. God asks us only to surrender ourselves, belong to him again each hour, and let him do the rest through us. This does not mean that we will not be involved with work, fighting, and pain. We have already seen that our life of prayer in Christ necessarily involves us in the cross. To the outsider it might seem to be a life of trial, sacrifice, and burdens borne for others, with many demands on our bodies and hearts. But we will find, in the midst of the pain and the burdens and the fighting, that we ourselves are at peace. It is God who wages the war through us, using our bodies and our personalities to bring about his will.

So let the beginner in prayer depend above all on the God of his prayer. When he is ready to move forward, God will prepare the way for him and give him the signal.

When he has mastered one step, he will be given another. When he has learned to understand one thing, he will be given another to learn. *To the extent that prayer is real to us, God will allow us to make it real to others.* If we try to go faster for others than we have for ourselves, we have stepped into unreality and outside the power which works in us.

At the beginning, when prayer and the Christ of prayer begin to become real to us, we must first pray that Christ himself will become our teacher and protector. This seems obvious, but it isn't. Many who are growing in prayer come under the spell of some strong, charismatic Christian leader or some powerful Christian movement. Instead of using these aids as *only* aids, we are apt to look to them as the ultimate strength and guidance themselves, rather than to the Christ from whom they come. An important illustration of this can be found in the book of Revelation, in which John, having received the vision, tries to worship the angel who brought it to him:

And when I heard and saw them, I fell down to worship at the feet of the angel who showed them to me; but he said to me, "You must not do that! I am a fellow servant with you and your brethren. . . . Worship God." (Rev. 22:8-9.)

It is hard *not* to worship those who have so helped us, prayed for us, given us of themselves, increased our vision, if by worship we mean ultimate gratitude, ultimate dependence. But to do so is disastrous for our spiritual growth and our very faith if the leader or helper shows us his weaknesses and faults, which he as a creature, certainly has.

It is even harder not to worship at the wrong place if one feels (as many sincere Christians do) guided by invisible helpers. There is certainly good evidence that communication can and does exist between the visible and invisible worlds. We state this faith publicly when we speak of the Church Triumphant which is united to the Church Militant. Many thoughtful Christians have believed and demonstrated this to be literal fact rather than mere inspiration and poetry. Nevertheless, though there be guidance and support and prayer for us beyond this world of the five senses, and though we may give thanks for it as we do for any guidance from our friends, we must commit ourselves ultimately only to God who comes to us through Christ. Only he can be our true teacher and our Way.

The next step is in no way contradictory. We pray for entrance into a group of Christians who understand the meaning of Christian prayer. There are many such people, but they are not always easy to find. They do not usually advertise themselves. They, too, depend on God to lead them to the people who need them. But remarks in casual conversation, in discussion groups, in books loaned and shared, in the special interests shown in their church life, will give us some indications who these people are. Some of these will be advanced, experienced Christians who are known to be already involved in prayer groups. Others will be beginners too. Still others will be potential believers

133

who do not realize that they are showing the signs of readiness for growth. Christ will bring us to these people if we ask him to, though it may be in completely unexpected ways.

A coming together of the concerned is the most natural way to begin a prayer group. There is nothing more deadly and hopeless than deliberately planned prayer groups organized and managed by the leaders of the church and thrust upon a half-prepared congregation. A group should arise naturally from a genuine awareness of need.

If it is the minister who is called to the life of prayer, he can discuss his faith with his deacons and invite those members of the church who are interested to join him in a regular place and time of prayer. He can speak of it from the pulpit, not with loud trumpetings but quietly, explaining the meaning of prayer as it now has come to him. He can invite those who have need of and interest in prayer to come together to form a nucleus of faith. Above all, he can quietly make it clear that he will be at a certain place at a certain time to pray regularly, whether anyone else can come or not. His congregation can depend on it that he will be there. Many will come, and a few will remain to become faithful members. And as time goes on, the church will increasingly turn to this group as a source of power and hope.

If it is a layman in the church who is called to prayer he can have a talk first with the minister. He may be surprised at the eager, almost wistful response. On the other hand, there may be a polite lack of response. In any

134

case, he can express his desire for regular meetings for prayer and name those who are also concerned. He can explain why and how this group is meeting and ask if the minister will go along with them to the extent of announcing that the group exists and is eager to help and welcome others. He should never try to pressure the minister into this way of prayer. But he should make clear his feelings that the church needs more prayer in its life and more life in its prayer. The minister should know that this group is supporting him and his ministry in its regular praying.

Many excellent books have been written on how to start and how to proceed with prayer groups. This book does not attempt to reiterate all the available advice and suggested methods. But whatever methods followed, and whether the group is a petitionary healing group or a meditating reading group; whether it meets in the church or in the homes; whether it remains the same faithful group for many years or has a rotating membership; whether it sits in silence, joins in special spoken prayers, or encourages spontaneous witness—the only thing that really matters is the same thing that really matters in the prayer life of the individual: the risen Christ who brings us God. The spark of life, the gift of the Spirit, the flow of strength are in his hand. Methods, organizations, plans, experiments, traditions, innovations are all pathetic gimmicks if we step outside the reality of this living Christ.

But we must remember that the group prayer, though extremely important, is not the only way to help the

135

church through prayer. If the believer does not feel called to organize or join a prayer group, he can pray for his church and its leaders individually. He can mentally hold the minister in the light of God through the sermon and pray that God will be enabled to touch many lives through the message. He can pray for the church boards and committees when they meet, praying that they may do the work of the church with integrity, vision, and generosity. He can pray for the church school teachers individually as they do their hard and often unrecognized important work. He can pray for the choir members as they sing, that they may be awakened to the living Christ while they sing his name.

Equally important is to pray for the outreaching work of the church: its missionaries, its charities, its shelters and homes for the handicapped and the aged. He can pray for those attending church or working on committees. It is especially important to hold in the light of God those persons who are chronic problems to the group in their inner tensions and anxieties.

Aside from actual prayer, he can remind others and witness lovingly and gently to the fact that the church exists as the unique group of men and women who celebrate their union with Jesus Christ, who still lives and brings us forever to God.

Far too often, those who are called to the life of prayer fall too easily into scorn for the church because of its neglect of prayer. That is the way out and a betrayal of the way God has chosen to hold and change his children.

After all, what is the church? We see the early concept of its meaning in the calling together of the Chosen People—the Hebrews. They were only a small, apparently insignificant group, in no way remarkable except for the fact that they had become aware of the calling of God and in response to that call had given themselves to him. Remember the poignant words of God spoken through Jeremiah to the Hebrews:

I remember the devotion of your youth, your love as a bride, how you followed me in the wilderness, in a land not sown. Israel was holy to the Lord, the first fruits of his harvest. . . . I thought you would call me, My Father, and would not turn from following me. (Jer. 2:2-3; 3:19*b*.)

Because, in the beginning, they had surrendered themselves in trust and depended on this merciful power of God for everything, a unique power had been created in that relationship between them and God. They were, indeed, a "holy people," because the word "holy" means set apart for special purposes. But whenever Israel turned away and broke the bonds of trust, their special relationship with their Source of being was betrayed and the special power was broken.

Eventually there was born into our world and history a man named Jesus, who was so utterly surrendered to the Father that there was no obstacle, no barrier at all between

137

him and God. A power such as the world had never seen before sprang into existence because of this perfect relationship between the Son and the Father. This power is what we call the Holy Spirit. It is an incredible torrent of living energy let loose into the world. It is a shaft of light that has penetrated all blackness and depth and hardness. When called upon, it can overcome anything—disease, fear, despair, ugliness, pain, hardness, all the black, cold chains which had kept us from the joy of the Father.

The group called into life and joy and strength by this power of the Holy Spirit is what the church was meant to be. Like Israel in the early days of its trust, it was called to be the obedient child, the radiant bride who followed God trustingly into the wilderness. Or to use Paul's analogy, it is called to be the Body of Christ visible in the world, surrendered to God, looking to him for everything, just as Jesus, the head of this Body, is the first man to be self-emptied and completely given to God. And the church's power for goodness is literally unlimited so long as it belongs to this man Jesus and is filled by the Spirit of his union with the Father.

You are a chosen race, a royal priesthood, a holy nation, God's own people, that you may declare the wonderful deeds of him who called you out of darkness into his marvelous light. Once you were no people but now you are God's people. (1 Peter 2:9-10.)

But it is not only for power and creativity that this relationship of trust and union is to be maintained. We

138

give our Creator, perhaps, ecstasy inconceivable when we surrender ourselves to him. It is the only thing we can give him. He does not need our works. He gives us the very strength by which we work, as well as the mind by which we think and the breath by which we live. He gives us everything we have. The only thing we can give him is our consent and our love. The only thing we can do for him is to say "yes" to him at every decision and challenge through the day. And our delight in surrendering to him is like a drop in the ocean of his delight when he receives our surrendered being. Remember again the words in Zephaniah, "He will rejoice over you with gladness, he will renew you in his love; he will exult over you with loud singing."

This is what the church was meant to be. A cup of joy to the Father. A body of power filled by the Spirit. It may undergo many changes in its present structure. The church organization a hundred years from now may be hardly recognizable to us. No matter. Change must come if the Spirit is present. But the basic meaning of the church will be unchanged. Lovers of God will meet together to express their love. They will know again in new ways that where two or three are joined together in the Real Presence, they will be filled with power and fire. No one called to prayer through Christ can hold aloof from this Body of commitment. Through him we must belong to it, heal it, and serve it with prayer without ceasing.

Epilogue

No book on prayer should leave the reader more anxious and burdened than he was before.

As we stop the reading and start the praying, we are invited to an experience of release. There are no rigid procedures laid down for prayer through Christ. There is no inflexible discipline, no required reading. We are not to sit anxiously reviewing our strong and weak points through a spiritual microscope. We are freed from all that.

We are praying now in the fresh air of the Good News. The News is that he loves us and can use us this minute exactly as we are. Our thoughts will wander, our resolutions will be vague, our indifference will often spread over us like a blight, but he can use us anyway if only we make the act of will in which we surrender ourselves and all our weaknesses to him. That is all he needs—our choice and our willing consent. It can begin now.

For the first time in our lives, perhaps, we can enter into the full joy and freedom of the Lord when we enter into prayer through the door of Christ.

140

According to our earliest historical records, men and women have prayed from the most primitive levels of civilization. Prayers have reached from the depths of animism to the heights of mystical union. We have reached out to respond to God and grope for him by many different methods and words. But in Christ, prayer is offered, for the first time, not as a striving but as a liberation.

This new way of praying is summed up clearly and pointedly by a Catholic educator writing for the Jesuit magazine *America:*

> Christian prayer is the prayer of Christ. . . . It is not an individual spiritual exercise, . . . it is not even the finest, best, and chiefest of all such exercises. It is a new exercise—not the prayer of natural man, but of the new man Christ Jesus. . . . It is not my prayer or your prayer, first of all, but the Lord's prayer, the Lord's praying in us and through us. . . . We enter into it. We climb aboard it. . . .
>
> The prayer of the church is the prayer of Jesus. It is already going on full tilt. It is not up to us to invent it, but only to join it. . . .
>
> We are free to pray badly, you see. The only thing we are not free to do is not to pray at all.[1]

In Christ there is no "praying type" anymore. We are freed from our moods and our temperament. By his liberating grace we are all, without exception, called to the ministry of prayer.

[1] Robert Farrar Capon, "The Secular and the Sacred," *America,* March 4, 1967, p. 311.

Suggested Reading

This list is not intended to be a complete bibliography of all the books on prayer that have helped me. It mentions merely a few of those I have valued in my growing. The reader will soon be able to compile his own list of books that reach him best in his own situation.

General

Day, Albert E. *An Autobiography of Prayer*. New York: Harper & Bros., 1952.

Heard, Gerald. A *Preface to Prayer*. New York: Harper & Bros., 1944.

Kelly, Thomas. A *Testament of Devotion*. New York: Harper & Row, 1941.

Lewis, C. S. *Letters to Malcolm: Chiefly on Prayer*. New York: Harcourt, Brace & World, 1964.

Magee, John. *Reality and Prayer*. New York: Harper & Row, 1957.

Mystical and Contemplative Prayer

Blakney, Raymond B. (tr. and ed.). *Meister Eckhart, a Modern Translation*. New York: Harper & Bros., 1941.

Cloud of Unknowing. Pendle Hill, Pennsylvania Publication, 1948.

Merton, Thomas. *Seeds of Contemplation*. Norfolk, Conn.: New Directions, 1949.

O'Brien, Elmer J. *Varieties of Mystic Experience*. New York: Holt, Rinehart & Winston, 1964.

Underhill, Evelyn. *Mysticism*. Cleveland, Ohio: Meridian Books (World Publishing Company), 1955.

Prayer of Healing and Wholeness

Neal, Emily Gardner. *God Can Heal You Now*. New York: Prentice-Hall, 1958.

Phillips, Dorothy B., *et al.* (eds.). *The Choice Is Always Ours*. New York: Harper & Row, 1960.

Weatherhead, Leslie. *Psychology, Religion, and Healing*. Nashville: Abingdon Press, 1951.

Prayer and the Christian Life

Day, Albert E. *Discipline and Discovery*. Baltimore, Maryland: Mt. Vernon Place Church, 1950.

Smith, Hannah W. *The Christian's Secret of a Happy Life*. New York: Grosset & Dunlap, Inc., 1958.

Underhill, Evelyn. *The Fruits of the Spirit, the Light of Christ, and Abba*. New York: David McKay Company, 1956.

Theological Background to Prayer

Baillie, John. *The Sense of the Presence of God*. New York: Charles Scribner's Sons, 1962.

Buber, Martin. *I and Thou*. New York: Charles Scribner's Sons, 1958.

Chesterton, G. K. *The Everlasting Man*. Garden City, N. Y.: Doubleday Image Book, 1955.

————. *Orthodoxy*. London: John Lane Company, 1908 (also: Garden City, N. Y.: Doubleday Image Book, 1959).

Teilhard de Chardin, Pierre. *The Divine Milieu*. New York: Harper & Row Torchbook, 1960.

Parapsychology and Psychical Research

Hart, Hornell. *The Enigma of Survival*. London: Rider & Company, 1959.

Johnson, Raynor. *The Imprisoned Splendour*. New York: Harper & Row, 1954.

Rhine, J. B. *The Reach of the Mind*. Clifton, N. J.: Apollo Editions, 1961.

Tyrrell, G. N. M. *The Personality of Man*. Baltimore, Maryland: Penguin Books, 1947.